Jesus in My Face takes you on a first hand journey through hell, from early teen years to mid-life, with a detailed, raw description of addiction. The author obviously possessed of good gifts physically and mentally, seems bent on self-destruction. But she desperately attempts, over and over to sober up and find meaning beyond parties and staying high. Despite relapse after relapse, she persists in seeking the answers to her addiction. The title of the book tells you where she found it. This book is worthy of a read for its insight into addiction, its lesson on perseverance, and its message to the hopeless – salvation is there for those who open their hearts to God.

—William C. Buhl, Circuit Judge Retired
Van Buren County, Michigan

Amy's story of self-imprisonment by the worst of addictions gives one a new understanding of the verse "God's truth will set you free." Her unabashed, honest testimony of a life lived in a downward spiral will inspire anyone who feels there is no hope. *Jesus in My Face* gives proof to the willing heart of God's transforming power.

—Ondalee Ashleman
Co-founder, Wings of God transition home

Amy, in a page-turning, soul-stirring book, identifies the characteristics and implications of one caught in addiction. She tells her story not as an observer, but as one who has battled the experience and has been victorious. As Amy shares her life and faith with family and friends, the reader is left with an overwhelming sense of hope and encouragement. Amy's book is a great read for anyone who needs to be assured of a better future and a transformed life. She does not offer simplistic or superficial solutions, but provides a powerful process by which others may know the health and the freedom that Amy now knows.

—Rev. Mark Vanderson
Senior Pastor, Southridge Reformed Church

Amy Atwater is as real as they come. She gives you a raw and honest look into a world only addicts know. What Amy has lived to tell about is proof that God has had His hand on her throughout her life. Amy's intelligence and zest for life will leave you at the end of the book wishing you could call her up and say, "Hey girl, let's go have coffee and talk."

—Elizabeth Frantz
Assistant Director of KPEP, an alternative to Jail

Jesus in My Face will change the eyes of an addict. No longer will they feel they are in a rut and have to stay. They will learn Jesus is within reach and will totally rock their world into healing of any addiction or dysfunction. This book speaks the raw truth of an individual who learned to be a professional addict and later tires of herself and reaches for Jesus and is changed for eternity! Addict or non-addict will find this book to be an incredible read. What an eye opener!

—Karina Lamorandier
Co-founder, Wings of God transition home

JESUS IN MY FACE

Ask... Seek... Knock !
(Matthew 7:7)

JESUS
IN MY FACE

A True Story
of Addiction and Redemption

Amy Atwater

TATE PUBLISHING
AND ENTERPRISES, LLC

Jesus in My Face
Copyright © 2013 by Amy Atwater. All rights reserved.

No part of this publication may be reproduced, stored in a retrieval system or transmitted in any way by any means, electronic, mechanical, photocopy, recording or otherwise without the prior permission of the author except as provided by USA copyright law.

Scripture quotations marked (NIV) are taken from the *Holy Bible, New International Version*®, NIV®. Copyright © 1973, 1978, 1984 by Biblica, Inc.™ Used by permission of Zondervan. All rights reserved worldwide. www.zondervan.com

Scripture quotations marked (NKJV) are taken from the *New King James Version*. Copyright © 1982 by Thomas Nelson, Inc. Used by permission. All rights reserved.

This book is designed to provide accurate and authoritative information with regard to the subject matter covered. This information is given with the understanding that neither the author nor Tate Publishing, LLC is engaged in rendering legal, professional advice. Since the details of your situation are fact dependent, you should additionally seek the services of a competent professional.

The opinions expressed by the author are not necessarily those of Tate Publishing, LLC.

Published by Tate Publishing & Enterprises, LLC
127 E. Trade Center Terrace | Mustang, Oklahoma 73064 USA
1.888.361.9245 | www.tatepublishing.com

Tate Publishing is committed to excellence in the publishing industry. The company reflects the philosophy established by the founders, based on Psalm 68:11,
"The Lord gave the word and great was the company of those who published it."

Book design copyright © 2013 by Tate Publishing, LLC. All rights reserved.
Cover design by Samson Lim
Interior design by Mary Jean Archival

Published in the United States of America

ISBN: 978-1-62295-452-0
1. Biography & Autobiography / Personal Memoirs
2. Biography & Autobiography / Religious
13.07.26

CONTENTS

Acknowledgments 9
Preface 11
Prologue: My Armageddon 15
Not My Bad.. 20
Meet the Parents... 27

Part 1 - Lost and Found

Happy Days 33
Dear Uncle 38
Child's Play.. 41
Missing Angel 47
Let's Make a Deal... 53
Tripped Out 59
Invisible 61
High School High 64
Hell-Bent-for-Leather 70
So Sue Me 80
Escape From the Zoo 82
Shattered 88
Joy and Mercy.. 96
Sin City 98
The Haunting 101

Special Delivery 107
Winter in Peru 116
The Mugging 119
Change is Good? 122
Single Mess 125
Simply Outrageous 130
Ken Doll 136
Third Time's a Charm 142
Not Celebrity Rehab 154
Rebirthing 161
Pure Love 165
Backsliding 170
Rolling, Rolling, Rolling 178
The Battle 181
Judge Not or Not? 192
Mighty Victory 196
Serve and Return 200
Totally Random 205

Part 2 - It's All About Jesus

Got Faith? 211
Sister Soul 216
Preach, Preacher! 224
Epilogue: Love Is… 232
Amy's Playlist 248

ACKNOWLEDGMENTS

To my parents, Bill and Rose Mary Glass, go my deepest thanks. I never lacked for food, clothing, shelter, and most especially love. Thanks for not giving up on me and doing your best to support and encourage me through my various valleys. You continually opened your door and hearts to me, never knowing what to expect next, but having faith, trusting in God, and believing in the power of prayer. Being a parent now, I finally realize the pain you have suffered for my sake.

Thanks to my mom and big brother Christopher, for editing my rough draft and supporting me with enthusiastic input. The opportunity to spend additional time with both of you was a blessed bonus to my project.

I would also like to acknowledge my daughter, Aubrey, for helping me in her own very important way; taking numerous dictations while I was behind the wheel whenever the Lord inspired me to write. Losing a thought can be highly frustrating and we can all use an extra set of hands sometimes. Thank you, sweetie!

A special thanks to all the pastors who have touched me with God's Word. First, from Southridge Reformed, I thank senior pastor Mark Vanderson and spiritual growth pastor Becky Ringler, who were largely responsible for opening my heart to hear the good news. Thanks, Charles Stanley, for your *Life Principles Daily Bible*. Thank you, Greg Laurie, for your *Daily Devotional*, and thanks to all of the awesome pastors who provide podcasts of their sermons: Charles Stanley, Greg Laurie, Mark Driscoll, Alistair Begg, Matt Chandler, Andy Stanley, James MacDonald, T. D. Jakes, Francis Chan, Creflo Dollar, Joyce Meyer, Chuck Swindall, Chip Engrim, Paul E. Shepard, James Dobson, Jon Weece, John Piper, Damon Thompson, David Jeremiah and all those I have failed to mention, and the pastors I have yet to discover. What a blessing the Internet can be! Thank you for your commitment to share the gospel truth.

Thanks to all the Christian music artists. There are far too many to name, and some are mentioned in the content and at the end of my book under "Amy's Playlist." I praise Christian radio stations, and I pray they will continue to grow and flood the airwaves with hope and encouragement. God-inspired music just keeps getting better. There is no end to the blessings you pour out on lost and wounded souls. Christian music has a way of penetrating the hardest of hearts. It is simply proof to me that the Holy Spirit is alive and well and in our midst.

Lastly, I thank my husband, Kenny, who has a heart of gold. He kept his promise to love me no matter what, and that is a mighty tall order. Thank you for loving Jesus and reintroducing him to me!

PREFACE

First of all, writing a book is nothing I ever dreamed of doing. I do not consider myself a writer, but I do have a story to share, all for the glory of God! I hope my testimony will serve as a witness to the exhaustive nature of my addiction; a long series of poor choices and setbacks, qualify how truly lost I was. Not that my entire life was one of total despair and tragedy; many have suffered far worse. I functioned highly, but the fact is, I was surrounded by chronic darkness. For many years I felt I had reached the point of no return. It was a long and tormented journey and I still spend a lot of time shaking my head in disbelief of the new creation I have become.

This book is a very personal and raw view into my life of deep seeded addiction, alcoholism, sexual immorality, and my eventual recovery. My intent is not to glamorize or glorify drug and alcohol use, but I would like to enlighten those who have been sheltered, naive, or perhaps may suffer from denial. Parents and loved ones of the afflicted will hopefully gain new insight into where the addicted mind can go, and there are so many opportunities to read between the lines.

I wish not to harm anyone in the process, especially my parents whom I have never blamed for a thing. They did the best they knew how. Besides, their unconditional love gave me the fortitude to keep pushing on.

My precious sister, Angel, as you will learn, tried my heart and wounded my soul with her actions and forgiving her did not come easily. I harbored deep resentments toward my sister for far too long, playing the blame game. Ultimately, I had to take full responsibility for what I had become. Without forgiveness, an essential element of my complete recovery, I would not be able to share with you my transformation. Angel is one of the strongest and most amazing people I know, and I have been called to support her through her trials. I love Angel with all my heart and am so proud to call her sister. It amazes me how she continues to overcome adversity in her life. As my dad puts it, "We are all suffering human beings."

I must not forget to mention that most names have been changed to protect the innocent and the guilty. Funny, my sweet big brother Christopher recommended I seek legal advice due to things I divulge about my past. As far as I know, I am beyond the statute of limitations, so I should be in the clear. Though hardly innocent, I am forgiven!

This book will be disturbing at times. My redemption involves transparency, and revealing my uncomely past has played a tremendous role in my recovery, and I recommend it to all who seek wholeness. I hope you can also find the irony and humor in it. God definitely has a sense of humor, along with a deep and unfailing love for his children. Come to find out, he was with me all the time.

The words to the song "Honestly" by Vota help to explain why it is imperative that I share my story.

> If you don't see my weakness
> You won't see what love has won…

My prayer is that you will connect to some portion of this book, and in doing so, the Holy Spirit convicts you to open your heart to a deepened understanding of his love. You too can discover true freedom.

Then you will know the truth, and the truth will set you free. (John 8:32 NIV)

PROLOGUE: MY ARMAGEDDON

Someone just shoot me! I thought. The end was drawing near. I could feel it. Drastic measures would have to be taken. I'd reached my bottom, at least I hoped and prayed that this was it. It had to be!

Demons of destruction were swirling through my brain, repeating that all too familiar mantra, "have another, have another, have another." Full blown spiritual warfare was raging inside me ever since I received Christ into my heart almost two years before. But I hid my torment so well; I was a master of deception. That's what three decades of alcohol and drug abuse will do. It was my career of sorts. Most people wimped out way before I did, they hit bottom, snapped out of the party life style, or wound up in jail. No, not I, my mind was twisted. It was in my blood!

I tried to remove my mask for family and friends over the years but the true depth of my soul sickness was not apparent to anyone. How could I describe something that I did not fully understand? Only the Lord knew what I was up against.

Satan had taken advantage of my foundation built on shifting sand. I once was a vulnerable child looking for relief from the dysfunction in our home. I chose the identity of extreme party girl very early on. This was how I coped. I found comfort there, but not anymore. My so-called best friend, the "almighty buzz," was fighting me to the finish. Was I doomed to die in a wasted haze? I'd rather be with Jesus now than go on living in this hell on Earth.

Webster's dictionary defines Armageddon as "a final and conclusive battle between the forces of good and evil." And so, my personal Armageddon occurred on Saturday, August 15, 2009, at approximately one a.m. The family reunion had ended, and everyone left late Friday afternoon.

I was drunk and stoned the entire ten days my family was present, which was not at all unusual. I planned to binge for the duration of their visit. Prior to the family reunion I enjoyed eleven weeks of sobriety. But I had little, if any, practice being sober around them, so I couldn't imagine it being any other way. My family was a huge trigger. I hoped it would be my last hurrah—I couldn't handle another relapse.

When my husband, Kenny, finally went to bed around eleven p.m. that Friday night, I was really jacked up. What used to be my favorite time of the day was now extreme torture. Free to get as plowed as I wanted, with no one to care, I slammed down a six-pack and smoked some more weed. I had already consumed my usual case of beer that day, something I'd been doing for months on end. It was not that difficult for me to do. I had a freakish tolerance.

I was sitting on the chaise lounge with my Bible in my lap and The Tennis Channel on mute, sobbing uncontrollably.

I began to pray, not unlike so many times before, looking up toward the heavens. "Dear Lord, when will it ever end? Why is quitting so difficult? Lord, if it is your will for me to live like this I don't know how much longer I can hang on! I love you no matter what, but please, Lord, give me a revelation, something, anything so I know what to do. I will quit for good this time. Just give me a sign. I need your help now, please, Lord, please. Am I going to die like this? Help me!"

This prayer came straight from the depth of my ravaged soul. The pain was excruciating. At that moment, in the pit, God spoke to me. It was not a still, quiet voice but a loud and clear, authoritative one. God said three simple yet profound words: "Write the book." I was floored at what happened, and I sat there, staring up, thinking, *What the…?*

God had just revealed himself to me in his mercy and I began to grin, while overcome by a mysterious warm glow and struck with a sense of peace and serenity. It was extraordinary, and I *knew* everything was going to be okay. With tears of relief streaming down my face, I said, "Yes, Lord, I will do it." God answered my prayer.

After a few awestruck moments, I jumped up and grabbed some scrap paper from the kitchen drawer, sat back down on the chaise lounge, and began writing. It was time to do a complete purge. As soon as I started putting all my random thoughts down on paper, I knew why God wanted me to write this book. My purpose, so evident, was to help save lost souls. I was to share my testimony, to witness to those struggling with addiction.

With paper and pencil in hand, I bolted to the kitchen and began puking in the sink, writing all the while. I attempted to drink another beer but was unable to keep it down. Hanging over the sink, I heaved, and wrote for the first half hour or so, purging my demons from deep within. Satan was vanquished, and my desire and cravings for drugs and alcohol evaporated. This was my final and conclusive *battle* with alcohol and drugs; *My Armageddon.*

I woke Kenny at three thirty a.m.—something I would never do normally—but he needed to be told. He was quite surprised when I told him that Pastor Mark Driscoll, and even the President, needed to hear the news. What happened to me was proof that our God reigns. How could I explain to Kenny my "orders from heaven" and how incredibly different I was? I desperately wanted him to understand.

Oddly, I started bleeding heavily that morning. I was a regular girl, and this period was two weeks early, and it came out of nowhere. I couldn't help but come to the conclusion that this was another sign from God, a type of sanctification, purification—being washed in the blood. I was now on a new monthly cycle.

I dumped the rest of my weed in the kitchen trash that morning, and as soon as Kenny got out of bed, I had him dispose of the last eleven beers; a professional drunk keeps a close inventory of their booze.

That very day, I called my parents and siblings to tell them that I was writing a book about my life because God told me to. My first phone call was to my sister Angel. She gave me her blessings, as did the rest of my family.

I spent the next five days wide-awake with a pencil and yellow legal pad in hand, filling almost a hundred and fifty pages. This was not a frustrating task even though I hated writing. Heck, I didn't pass an English class after seventh grade. This was a huge stretch for me, to write a book, but I could not stop pouring out my thoughts and memories. The floodgates were wide open, and the guilt and shame of my past were diminishing with every stroke of the pencil.

NOT MY BAD

Unfortunately, Kenny was not picking up on the significance of what occurred the week prior, so I asked my two best friends, Roxy and Lauren, to come over and, unbeknownst to them, mediate a discussion. They had witnessed the changes in me since my stay at *Jim Gilmore Treatment Center* (rehab) and my conversion a couple of years before. They were supportive of my writing and believed me when I told them what happened. I had confided in them so many times over the years about the misery I was living in. I was one of the sanest people they knew, albeit with an army of demons. Kenny, on the other hand, was leery. He was bitter and doubtful "the book" would mean anything to anyone or that it was a gift from God. He made the point during the meeting that I was one of many addicts to write a book. Why would mine be different? He didn't believe I had a revelation, apparently. Why would I lie, and where was his faith? He didn't understand addiction or feel it necessary to attend any Al-Anon meetings to educate him after I entered rehab. Kenny was a very busy man and had suffered from a roller-coaster ride from my numerous relapses since our marriage in October 2006. Almost three years of broken promises had led him to a great deal of confusion. It was a miracle he hadn't dumped me, really.

Even still, I was upset by his remarks and apparently hadn't got it all out in our discussion with my friends. After we climbed into bed that night and Kenny was fast asleep I began stewing over his negativity and composed a letter to him.

> Ken,
>
> It may be best if we just say our good-byes. This book and my sobriety are more important to me than suffering with the additional pain and guilt of trying not to disappoint you. I have enough on my plate, and the fact that you don't understand adds an ungodly amount of unneeded and unwanted stress and pressure.
>
> Maybe leaving you would be just the thing you need to help you look inside yourself and make the changes you need to be a better husband… But no, that's right, you're perfect. You grew up spoiled rotten with a spoiled rotten attitude about people. I don't need you to stay sober. I only need Jesus and to get my book published. Then I can do what I want with it without having to worry about what you think all the time. Life is too short. I can leave you. The pain of leaving you will pale in comparison to the past pains and current stress that I'm under to write this book to save the remaining good years I have left. Forget you for not trying harder to understand. You're a self-righteous, self-centered SOB who judges others. I will fulfill my dreams with or without you. Do

you think leaving you would be any harder than divorcing Timothy or Juan? Think again. It would be a cake walk for me. Trust me. Divorcing me would make you a better man. Who knows, maybe in a few years we will reunite. But three years of sobriety probably won't be enough for you, and the possibility of a relapse is always looming. You need someone as perfect as you. I need someone who's sinned a little more that will not pass judgment because you can't understand where I'm coming from. Get off my back, or I will leave. You, on the other hand, will be kicking yourself in the rear the rest of your life.

Your bad, not mine!

We made a mistake. Shall we just move on? I knew I should have never married again until I got well, but I never will be well anyway because I am an addict and we relapse. Sorry for ever marrying you and any pain I've caused. You may get over it, but I will always have my cross to bear. I know you can do so much better than me.

I punched Kenny in the arm, shoved the letter in his face, and escaped to the living room, slamming the door behind me.

—⚋—

I had pushed Kenny to his limit. He was tired of walking on pins and needles, never knowing if I'd be stoned and slamming beers when he returned home from work. I could hide the cocaine and meth fairly easily, and what he didn't know wouldn't hurt him. I isolated a lot and was drinking way more than Kenny would ever know. Lord knew, he wanted this ride to end and when I entered rehab in September, 2007, it was an answer to his prayers.

Regrettably, rehab was not the end all. I relapsed again and again and again. I was losing hope and decided to try Antabuse. I'd been attending the *Community Healing Center* for outpatient therapy once a week after I got out of rehab, and had heard about Antabuse during a class. This medication somehow helped alcoholics abstain. I decided to look into it.

It was nearly impossible for me to make it to an AA (Alcoholic Anonymous) meeting every day after I opened the salon in Lawton, which no doubt, would have kept me sober.

My doctor wrote me a prescription. I hated having to take any prescribed medications. I rarely took aspirin for that matter, but the urge to drink overwhelmed me no matter how hard I prayed. I would try anything at this point to quit drinking.

I thought Antabuse was a miracle drug; a gift from God in the beginning. I was having planned drunks: three to seven weeks on it and a weekend off. Roxy made the comment that she didn't know it was supposed to be used that way. It wasn't, but I found a way to abuse it. I was just being me. Satan was so sneaky.

Come to find out, Antabuse was a very dangerous drug for this alcoholic, having had two nightmarish episodes. I was only taking half the prescribed dose and stopped taking the pills for two days prior, in preparation for drinking, figuring that would be enough time to get the Antabuse out of my system. The first time was after a tennis drill in the "Zoo." I picked up a six-pack (I was going to drink in moderation that day) and sucked down a couple before going into the tanner. While in the hex, I became lightheaded and had to sit down before my time was up. I made it to the car and headed home to Lawton, a half hour drive away, thinking I could shake it off. I barely made it, praying the entire way.

It was reminiscent of hallucinogens. Objects breathed and the road had waves in hues of purple and orange. I was losing control of my motor skills, barely able to keep my head up, well aware of what was happening. I couldn't do anything about it and was shocked at the side effects. What kind of cruel joke was this? It was the worst trip I had ever been on. That's saying a lot if you take into account the hundreds of times I'd tripped before. Jim Morrison had nothing on me. I was expecting, if anything, a sick-to-my-stomach, flu-like reaction. I wish someone would have warned me. I *might* have waited until I got home that day to drink. I could not figure out why this drug was prescribed to alcoholics.

A few months later, I had a couple of beers and went to my stepson's better-late-than-never high school graduation party at his mom's house just a few blocks away. I was nervous about going to Kenny's ex-wife's place, or at least that was my excuse, so I backed off of the Antabuse two days before. I started having a reaction and told Kenny I was running home for a minute. I never returned. I pulled up in front of our home, got out, and collapsed on the sidewalk in front of the door. It was in broad daylight. I paused for a moment and crawled up the steps to the door, stood up, opened the door, and collapsed again in the foyer and slithered to the bedroom. What a horrible feeling, being of sound mind and having little control over my body. I called Kenny after I got up into bed. He was not angry, just worried about me. He was fully aware of the first episode, so he wasn't shocked. He stopped by to check up on me, and then returned to the party while I stayed in bed and rode the waves. I continued to take Antabuse because it was the only way I could stay sober at the time.

So as you can see, from just a small sample, Kenny had the right to be leery about my new endeavor. How could he trust anything I said after all the times I'd let him down. This poor man was so patient and loving, and our relationship had been a powerful test of his faith.

Shockingly, Kenny came to my rescue that night after reading my angry letter. This was something he had never done before. I'd spent countless nights sobbing on the chaise lounge in the living room, frustrated after Kenny went to bed, praying he would come and comfort me.

But that night we had a very long and calm discussion about the current circumstances. Something amazing had come over him; clearly, another answered prayer. He was a changed man. The Holy Spirit set him straight, and I had his full, loving support; not an ounce of doubt or cynicism left in him. The letter was a gift from God.

Shortly after, Kenny bought me my very own notebook laptop just for writing my book. I never would have dreamed it, bless his heart. Too bad I didn't know how to type, a testament to God's sense of humor. Hunting and pecking this book was perhaps the most challenging part of the entire process. At the very least, the Lord was using it to teach me patience.

MEET THE PARENTS

I feel it is appropriate to seize this opportunity to honor my parents with a brief description of their background as an attempt to exalt them for putting up with my very slow rate of maturation. This is also proof that I was not raised by mental midgets. Intelligent, well-meaning, and loving parents can have horribly rotten children. I'd be one of them.

My father, William Thomas Glass, was adopted in 1931 and grew up working in the family furniture business. At age twenty, after sailing the Great Lakes, serving in the navy, he enrolled at what is now Western Michigan University. While on a visit to Notre Dame's campus, he was inspired to enroll in the fine arts program there. While earning his bachelor's and master of fine arts degrees, he studied sculpture with Ivan Meštrović and was first assistant to Mexican Renaissance mural painter Jean Charlot. In graduate school, he taught classes at both Notre Dame and nearby St. Mary's College. In the late fifties, he joined Rookwood Pottery in Cincinnati, Ohio, America's most famous producer of art pottery. He's the last formally trained Rookwood artist as well as the last surviving artist.

In the late sixties, Dad designed and patented—of all things—a safety ashtray, SAFTI-PLUS. It clearly showed his design skills. I grew up with all kinds of Dad's interesting ashtray creations. He smoked cigarettes for a short time, in part, to test his creations, but he never inhaled. He also smoked a pipe for many years. I loved to hang around him when he smoked his pipe, fascinated with the smell of the sulfur from the matches and the large plumes of smoke.

Dad is not only an artist, but a born salesman. To make ends meet, he sold anything from vacuums to chemicals and, eventually, chose a career in real estate in the late seventies.

In the late eighties, Dad returned to art, focusing on art pottery and large-scale sculpture and is currently putting out some of his best work in retirement. I am very proud of all his contemporary works and a good example would be *Katrina*, which he created in 2007, after the hurricane along the Gulf Coast. It is a fabulous piece to study with its many twists and turns.

Dad has numerous sayings and jokes he has repeated often throughout the years, and I have to admit many have rubbed off on me. I am my father's daughter. His favorite recitation when he has an audience, and he loves an audience—would be the Fisherman's Prayer.

> God grant that I may fish
> Until my dying day…

My favorite hyperbole of Dad's is "I'm so hungry I could eat the rear end out of a snake." It really grossed me out as a kid. "Go play in busy traffic," "I've got an aunt who can't sing either," "Amy Clare Glass is a pain in the ass," and "Do you know how to get rid of ten pounds of ugly fat? Chop off your head." These are just a few of his sayings. He always said them in the most loving way. Dad's a beautiful artist, dreamer, entrepreneur, and fun-loving guy, and he will always be famous in my mind.

My mother, born Rose Mary Oberski, was born in 1936 in Parisville, Michigan, one of the oldest Polish settlements in the United States. Polish is her first language. Mom is the oldest of five children. She was a legal secretary when my parents met and married in 1957. She earned a Bachelor of Arts degree with a major in Spanish and minor in Russian while helping raise us and run the family business. Mom graduated summa cum laude from Western Michigan University in 1976 at age forty. She always worked in addition to being a mother and soon embarked on a new career. Mom became the director of communications for a third-party health plan administrator. In addition, Mom was active in women's networking and served on the board of the YWCA. She retired in 1999.

Mom's a brilliant woman who excels in language, writing, poetry, and child rearing. She certainly has a gift with words, and after Dad produced the *Katrina* sculpture, she wrote the following:

> Katrina
>
> Like a multi-headed beast, Katrina
> lunged toward the land breathing fury.
> Her ravenous, tortuous waves ferociously
> lapping against the Gulf Coast shore
> swallowing up all that stood before,

spitting out detritus in her wake
…and misery.
In her dark wrath, the daughter
showed no favor or mercy,
like Mother Nature taught her.
For the Earth knows neither
malice nor beneficence
and shrouds its ways in mystery.
As for the toll of suffering and pain
incompetence and indifference must bear the blame.

That's good stuff although I have to admit I had to look up a few of the words. I have a folder labeled "Insights" that I've added to for over twenty years, and it is full of Mom's poetry and writings, all of them thought provoking.

Mom and Dad never stopped being my educators—from Dad throwing vocabulary words at me throughout the years to them both watching and discussing numerous local and national newscasts and our favorite show, *60 Minutes*. I cherish those times we spent together.

I was blessed with well-rounded genes. Like my father, I enjoy having fun with people and working with my hands. Writing a book is something that my mother would do, and I am only able to do, by the grace of God. It's *so* not me.

PART 1
LOST AND FOUND

HAPPY DAYS

In the beginning we were your normal middle class, church going family. Everything was as it should be, I suppose, for a family of seven.

I was born in Starkville, Mississippi, on November 7, 1965. Mom and Dad moved from Cincinnati, Ohio, in 1961 when Rookwood Pottery relocated. One of my earliest memories was at The Gift Gallery, which Dad established soon after arriving in Starkville. Dad taught classes, exhibited regional artists' works, retailed art supplies, and made custom frames there. Mom and Dad ran the business, so I made frequent visits with them to eat the sugar cubes on the coffee cart and "help" Dad make frames.

We had a nanny, Dorothy, who helped Mom with the task of raising five children. Dad always said, "Five's not a record, but it ain't no hobby either." Mom actually had seven pregnancies in seven years with two miscarriages. I am the last born. After my birth, the doctor told Mom that her body needed a rest from pregnancy, or it could be harmful to her health.

Mom and Dad were born and raised Catholic, which made the decision of birth control difficult. They certainly weren't going to quit having sex (my dad's nickname in school was "Six-hands Glass"), so birth control was the best solution. My oldest brother and sister, Christopher James and Sissy, are Polish twins born less than a year apart. Angel was born two years later, and a couple years after that came Danny. I was due on Danny's first birthday and arrived two days late, so you could consider Danny and me Polish twins as well.

Our vacations were spent traveling the country in a VW bus, hitting amusement parks and visiting historic sites and museums. It was a free-for-all in the back of that bus, Dad frequently saying, "If I have to pull over…!" It was usually because someone was picking on poor, innocent little me—Amy. I don't think that my siblings picked up on the fact that I was *beloved*, the meaning of my name.

I have fond memories of the five of us walking to the local store for an ICEE. I was in love with that ICEE polar bear, but Pooh was my favorite bear of all; hence, one of my nicknames was Piglet, lovingly given to me by my big brother, Christopher. I'm sure it had nothing to do with the fact that I was plump.

I had a love affair with Winnie-the-Pooh for many years. My dad once had to turn the bus around and return to Disneyland because I lost my brand-new Pooh. He was a sucker for my crocodile tears. I loved all the fur right off that bear. When Danny ripped off Pooh's arm, Mom had to sew it back on; and when he tried to rip off his head, it was Mom to the rescue.

Danny and I shared some good times. We used to spin each other around in an old office chair because our legs were too short for us to do it on our own. I loved spinning; it was an instant buzz.

We also shared a bedroom and some not so good times. I remember Danny hitting me when I rocked and rhythmically bounced my face in the pillow at night, making odd noises while he was trying to sleep next to me. I couldn't blame him. Oftentimes, in the wee hours of the morning, to avoid the angry outbursts from my brother, I would go to the living room to rock on the couch. I busted most of the springs out of the back of that couch and they went right through the plaster wall. The holes, of course, were discovered well after the fact, probably during a thorough cleaning of the house or an attempt at rearranging the furnishings. I was busted! I guess you could say I was a born rocker.

In our bedroom hung a lovely drawing of a dark-skinned baby peeking out from under a blanket, which was a gift to my mother from Jean Charlot, himself. Danny used to tell me that it was me in the drawing, and that I was born black, unlike the rest of my family. At that time, it was very upsetting, and my parents had to reassure me that sweet little Danny was just teasing.

On top of that, I spoke with a lisp and was incessantly teased by my siblings. Try saying *Mithithippi* with your tongue hanging out; not very funny. The character-building opportunities were plentiful and darn near never ending. I was easy pickings!

My big brother, Christopher, also loved to tease me about the "permanent Kool-Aid ring" around my mouth. It was already apparent I had a drinking problem. Then there was my least favorite nickname,

Scabby Appleton, because of the massive quantities of mosquito bites that I scratched and picked until they were bloody. Christopher punched me in the arm as hard as he could one time when he was trapped next to me on a trip and I was picking. He couldn't stand the sight of blood. My bad!

My mother sewed a good bit of our clothes, and I loved shopping for the patterns. The culottes she made were the greatest. I treasured all of Mom's creations, but none like the long gold velvet dress for cousin Bill's wedding. It was the one and only time I was a flower girl, and I never wanted to take it off; I wore this dress until the seams were bursting. Mom always worked hard to dress us properly, and Easter Sunday was always the main event.

Mom made a sit-down dinner for seven, every day of the week for years. Dad always led us in saying grace and often ended it with, "Lord, come through the roof, and I'll pay for the shingles." He loved to make us laugh.

Mom sometimes did the grocery shopping with all of us in tow. Imagine going with five young children aged ten to three. You are on a mission and in a hurry so as not to prolong the agony. You check out, load the groceries in the car, and drive off with a sigh of relief. You get home and start unloading the groceries, and the phone rings:

"Mrs. Glass, did you forget anything at the store today?"

Mom inspects the groceries and replies, "No, it looks like I have everything."

The cashier says, "We have a little girl here that says she belongs to you."

I'm certain Mom was horrified. A mother can only do so much. I wonder how long before Mom, or anyone else for that matter, would have noticed I was missing if she had not received the phone call.

My father had wonderful taste in decorating due to his background and interest in modern art. Our home interior showed his flare. While at Notre Dame he created several depictions of the crucifixion and they adorned the walls in our home. I loved to touch and study this man Jesus who hung on the cross.

The house was full of contemporary furnishings and various works of modern art as well. Mom was a farm girl with little exposure to the arts, so Dad had to "educate" her. "She never wore shoes 'til I met her," so he joked, and he preferred to keep her barefoot and pregnant anyway. Seriously, my father was always my mom's biggest fan, and he even encouraged her to take assertiveness classes. Dad was no male chauvinist.

Dad called me his "star," when I was little and the power of his words, no doubt, helped me survive throughout the years. I was blessed to have an extremely loving and supportive earthly father. "Daddy, carry me" was my famous line for many years. I didn't learn how to walk until I was ten years old, because my father carried me everywhere, so my family liked to joke.

DEAR UNCLE

I seemed to have a knack for getting myself into trouble, like when I got caught putting our new kitten, Tinker Bell, in the toilet to see if she could swim. Not to mention, the two times I drowned at our local YMCA between the ages of three and four. All my siblings were great swimmers, and then there was me. I had no concept of drowning and decided one day that I could swim too, so I jumped into the deep end and quickly sank to the bottom. Dad rescued and revived me the first time. The second time, I was playing in the shallow end (no longer allowed in the deep end) and tempting fate, went too close to the deep end and slid to the bottom. A lifeguard rescued me, and again, the water had to be pumped out of my lungs. Dad's saying "Amy Clare Glass is a pain in the ass" oftentimes rang true!

My most terrifying memory when we lived in Mississippi actually happened while visiting Grandma and Grandpa Glass for their fiftieth wedding anniversary in Harbor Beach, Michigan. On this particular visit we stayed with Grandma and Grandpa Oberski, who lived a few miles away in Parisville, Michigan.

Grandpa and Grandma Oberski owned a combination hotel and bar with numerous rooms upstairs, so we often slept in our own room. This particular night, Danny was not feeling well so he got to take a couple of Bayer baby aspirins. It's like candy, right? I loved that stuff, and Mom wouldn't let me have any no matter how hard I begged.

Well, I found an opportunity while everyone was asleep and grabbed the just-opened bottle of baby aspirin off of Danny's nightstand. I took it downstairs to the family room and ate the remaining aspirin.

Uncle Gary was up very early that morning for high school football practice. He was fifteen-years-old and my favorite uncle. Uncle Gary loved to tease me, and I thought he was funny. He used to tell me I had poop-brown eyes because I was full of poop up to here, as he put his hand up to his forehead.

I was on the couch, rocking and sucking on the cap and had hidden the bottle in the cushions to dispose of the evidence. He was a sweet boy and cared enough to notice I had something in my mouth. When he discovered it was the lid of the Bayer aspirin bottle, he questioned me and I said nothing. He proceeded to check the cushions and, lo and behold, found the empty bottle and woke up the entire house.

Grandma Oberski called the hospital, which was far away, and they said to give me water. Their water was nasty. It was like drinking from the ocean. I didn't even like to brush my teeth with it. They rushed me to the hospital where the doctor shoved a tube down my throat and pumped my stomach. I still can recall the orange shooting up the tube as I was being restrained. This was my first close call with a drug overdose at age four.

Uncle Gary was an angel, and I was forever thankful for him. Tragically, he died seventeen years later at the age of thirty-two in a small-plane accident. The crash occurred in Kalamazoo, Michigan, where we lived at the time. We think he may have been coming to surprise my mom. I found it a bit uncanny that he saved my life and lost his prematurely in my "backyard," so to speak. He was a successful accountant and left behind a wife and three small children.

CHILD'S PLAY

My best friend and first love was a boy I met in preschool. His name was Christopher too, just like my big brother. We were the very best of friends for two years. We hung out at recess, stomping on and eating pecans that had fallen on the playground and kissed behind the big empty wire spools we used for finger painting. He was my first real connection to someone outside my family.

Sadly, our family moved to Michigan in the summer of 1971. I was devastated to leave Christopher, but Dad's SAFTI-PLUS ashtray was manufactured in Mendon, Michigan, and moving got us closer to his business, as well as my grandparents, who were getting up there in age.

Not long after we moved to Michigan, my mom and dad received a phone call from Christopher's parents. They called to share the horrific news that Christopher had passed away. I'd already experienced my first broken heart when we moved, and now I was mourning the loss of a loved one for the first time. Leaving Mississippi was bad enough, but why did Christopher have to die? I convinced myself that he died of a broken heart because I moved to Michigan, and that's what I declared to my mom and dad, and it wasn't far from the truth. Christopher died because he had a hole in his heart. Pooh sure came in handy for that trauma. I worked Pooh over pretty good, and he suffered substantial hair loss.

―⁓―

My first November in Michigan, I remember looking out the kitchen window and praying to God for snow on my birthday. In Mississippi, I'd seen flurries once or twice, but the snow hit the ground and melted. I wanted the real deal for building snowmen, sledding, and having snowball fights. I woke up on my birthday, and it was snowing hard, and we wound up getting four to six inches. I was thanking God all day long for answering my prayer and enjoyed all I had been dreaming of and more. We had a large hill in the backyard and a toboggan that fit all five of us. I sat in between Christopher's legs, the safest place to be, and we had the time of our lives.

Our new home was in the heart of Western Michigan University's student housing, one of the few single-family houses left in the area. It was surrounded by apartment complexes and a large expanse of woods with a park beyond the end of our street that contained Hawkins Pond, a playground, baseball fields, and a picnic area. And to top it off, there were train tracks off in the distance.

Danny and I especially enjoyed playing on the tracks, testing how brave we were when trains were approaching. We spent hours hunting for fossils and defacing coins on the tracks. The hard part was finding the flattened coins after the trains crushed them, and luckily, we didn't lose any eyes after they shot off the tracks.

We collected pussy willows and cattails. We picked red and black raspberries and brought them home by the bowlful. The thorns were not a deterrent. The rewards outweighed the wounds. We also found numerous "treasures" for Mom dumpster diving at the apartment complexes.

We had a large wooden box on our back patio that we used for captured critters. Danny and I loved to hunt for snakes and caught dozens over the years; garter snakes were the most common. I took a garter snake to show-and-tell to demonstrate a snake bite. I'd been bitten so many times, that it barely fazed me. I got the snake to bite me and let it hang from my finger, removed him, and showed the class the tiny marks. I don't think the teacher was expecting that, but my classmates loved it!

Hawkins Pond was always an adventure. Danny and I fished it, skated on it, and sailed on it when we found half of an old oil tank that was sufficiently seaworthy. We each had a large stick that allowed us to navigate the water. Snapping turtles enjoyed grabbing our sticks and that was surely the highlight of those excursions. I had a couple of run-ins with Danny's fishhooks when he was casting. One hook was embedded in my wrist, and another time, one got stuck in my thumb. Our solution was for Danny to rip them out. It worked rather well, and he didn't mind doing it. Stuff happens.

Back to fishing, just a little farther down shore from Danny. He was never eager to take the fish off my hook, and he especially enjoyed watching me get stung by the catfish and bullhead. He finally gave in one day and showed me the trick, probably because I was crying.

We also enjoyed hunting frogs with our BB guns down at the Hawkins Pond (easy pickings). When we ran out of ammo we packed our BB guns with sand and shoot each other at point-blank range. We came home with bruises resembling large purple tie-dye. The sand hurt more than the BBs. Looking back, we were just plain rotten, and our poor mother was often distressed by our conduct. *Rug rats* did not begin to describe us.

—☆—

Stealing didn't seem like such a bad thing to do, either. Danny and I discovered a couple of fountains on the WMU campus. We waded in them to take the money. We rode the elevator to the top floor of one of the buildings on campus and discovered a lounge, and we stole the donated coffee money. I was caught the first time I shoplifted at our local "Stop and Rob." I walked out with a pair of wax lips, my favorite thing at the time, and was quickly apprehended, but eventually let go and banned from the store. Danny and I continued to steal, moving on to bigger and better things. Boy oh boy, if Mom and Dad had only known.

When I wanted more cerebral stimulation I'd hangout with my big brother, Christopher. We spent untold hours together in his bedroom, playing games—chess, Stratego, Risk, Mastermind, and Battleship, to name a few. He was very patient and an excellent teacher. When it came to Danny and me borrowing a game though, he was always a tough sell. I never understood why; we were such *reserved* kids.

I shared a bedroom with Sissy and Angel—three twin beds in one small room. I witnessed some nasty fights between my sisters there. Angel was becoming difficult, and apparently, there was a lot more going on than your usual teenage-girl stuff.

Angel got into a bad crowd and began abusing drugs and I was not feeling the love from her anymore. She treated me as though I was the enemy. My philosophy was to keep my distance, but on the other hand, I wanted her favor like any little sister would, and I set myself up for some major upsets.

Our happy home life was over. We were all forced to deal with what was happening in Angel's life. She quickly sucked the fun out of our family. The dysfunction could not be ignored.

It was an extremely confusing time in my life, and the more she lashed out at me the more defiant and withdrawn I became. I was spending a substantial amount of my down time alone in the basement playing solitaire and rocking in my chair, listening to the radio, memorizing the words to every song. Music was my great escape.

My parents were struggling financially. As Dad put it, "I'm up to my ass in alligators,"—a saying I have to admit I heard far too often. Dad was working on the ashtray business, selling vacuums and other household products just to keep a roof over our heads while Mom was in school full-time, studying for her bachelor's degree.

We had some rough years when garage sales clothed us, and my parents went without pleasures, not even as much as a six-pack of beer. I also remember powdered milk. They did what they had to do, all while trying to keep Angel in line.

MISSING ANGEL

Angel became highly rebellious at about age thirteen, refusing to do her chores and exhibiting deviant behavior. I called her the "B" word one day, and my mother overheard and dragged me by the arm to the kitchen and threatened to wash my mouth out, with bar of soap in hand.

There'd been a lot of chaos in the house for the last several months, and it was apparent Christopher had had enough. He was so fed up with Angel that he threw her down the stairs along with the vacuum cleaner. Angel was not acting logically, and you didn't mess with Spock, from *Star Trek*, whom Christopher emulated.

Angel was continually getting into trouble, still hanging out with a bad crowd, doing drugs, and skipping school. She was hateful and abusive. She wore steel-toed boots as a rule, great for kicking any little kid that got in her way. I was most definitely scared of Angel. I walked in on her smoking a cigarette in the laundry room, and she burned me with it, handed it to me, and made me take a puff. I was nine-years-old, and she was fourteen. She told me she'd kick my butt if I told Mom and Dad. Angel burned me on a number of occasions for kicks and giggles, always threatening to beat me up if I told. Fear had entered my life like never before. I couldn't tell on Angel; I knew she'd make good on her promise. Plus, we slept in the same room. I couldn't risk telling my mom and my dad. I would have to figure this out on my own. How could they protect me? They had their hands full with Angel. She was completely out of control.

I was minding my own business one day, down in the basement, listening to the radio and rocking in a chair, where I liked to go to get away from the constant stress. Angel came down holding a flashlight with no batteries in it and asked me to blow in it. I knew she was up to something, but she insisted. I did, and my eyes were filled with corroded battery rust. I was devastated she would do that to me and laugh. It was just another random act of cruelty. She was evil, and *I* was easy pickings. I had no recourse and so I continued to keep these horrible secrets. I was living in fear of Angel on a daily basis, and you could cut the tension in our home with a knife.

I started having a recurring nightmare and was afraid to go to sleep. I had this nightmare at least a dozen times and would wake up crying. The Wicked Witch of the West was chasing me. I discovered that I could wake myself up, and that was great, but it didn't stop the nightmare from coming. I had a plan. When it happened again, I would stand firm and kick that witch's butt. The last time I had that horrible dream, I was very brave; and as the wicked witch approached me with her gnarly green hands out ready to grab me, I simply slapped them, and she disappeared. It was the end of that witch.

Unfortunately, Mom and Dad were beside themselves with their own little wicked witch. Angel had already been in and out of juvenile detention twice for truancy and drug use by the age of fourteen. Danny and I were questioned by the judge about our situation at home before she was popped from juvy the second time, but we were both too scared to say much of anything.

Angel was not allowed to leave the house without a chaperone now, because she was on probation. Mom and Dad weren't home this particular afternoon and she insisted I go to the park with her so she wouldn't get in trouble. She would *not* take no for an answer, if you can imagine. I soon found out this was a hangout for all her druggy friends. There were four or five guys sitting on some steps, smoking and drinking, and one of the guys handed Angel some pills. She took a couple and handed me one. She was up to her old tricks, so I took it. She said it was a Valium, and that I'd like it. She also made me take a hit from a joint and take a swig of beer. I was just ten-years-old. I never went to the park with Angel again. I don't remember going home. I suppose I returned in a fog. No doubt, I was back to the basement, as soon as possible, hanging with my friend, the radio.

My parents were taking Angel to the Child Guidance Clinic for counseling, but things were getting worse. Angel was living deep in her teenage wasteland. As Angel got a little older, say sixteen, so did the guys she ran with. She became much more intimidating and made frequent threats on our lives, and we were all downright scared. We became captives in our own home. She'd walk into the house with her thug friends and steal whatever she wanted, including my parents' money. She regularly ransacked the house and my dresser drawers. One instance, she stole a brand-new shirt of mine. I was saving it for a special occasion—the Kansas's Leftoverture concert. She actually had the nerve to wear it to that concert, and I could see her from my seat. She was front and center, trying to climb over the barricade to get onstage. She was obviously out of her mind. I watched her get carried off the floor, and she wound up being thrown out. I eventually got the shirt back, snagged and torn.

I remember Angel coming into the house when Danny, Mom, and I were hanging out in the kitchen. We all just kind of froze, never knowing what to expect. It was like living in a nightmare. She grabbed a pizza from the freezer, turned the electric stove burner on high, and flipped it upside down onto it. Yikes! She was as usual—angry, cussing, and belligerent.

There was no communicating with Angel. Her group of friends was getting into some even more frightening drugs. Angel was smoking Crazy Flakes, a mixture of marijuana, embalming fluid (formaldehyde), and PCP (poison), glue for sniffing, and nitrous oxide. It seemed as though she had really fried some brain cells. As a last-ditch effort to get her some help, my mom and dad sent Angel to a mental institute for an evaluation. She was in a lock-down facility with wrought-iron bars on the windows. This was where she belonged from my perspective. Unfortunately, she had everyone fooled except me. I knew Angel like nobody ever would. She manipulated her way out in a few weeks and was free. The system failed my mom and dad. They had exhausted all their avenues. Even if they could have afforded a long-term mental health facility, Angel's lack of diagnosis would not have supported it. I remember my feelings of anxiety and shock when she was released so quickly.

I can't begin to imagine the pain my parents were going through. How my mom and dad made it through those years, Lord only knows.

I was not going to do to them what Angel had done. Instead of choosing a life free of drugs, I decided I could use drugs and alcohol and be really smart about it because what they didn't know wouldn't hurt them, and *I* could keep it under control. If you can't beat 'em, join 'em, was my attitude. My fear of Angel eventually turned into anger.

But I couldn't help but feel horrible for Angel sometimes. There were nights when she would come into our bedroom and wake me up just to interrogate me if she wanted something, and other nights she would climb in bed with me and cry and hold me tight. It was creepy. My sister was truly demonized. When I looked at her, I wondered if she was even in there.

She had been beaten and brutally raped more than once; and unfortunately, I witnessed the aftermath. Once dumped on our curb in front of our house, she crawled to the door, bloody, beaten, and sobbing. A particular boyfriend (term used loosely) drove a van with a mattress in the back for gangbanging girls after they were wasted. These boys were sadistic and Angel was not the only victim. Mom and Dad tried pressing charges but got nowhere. Angel suffered so much trauma that she was unable to remember what happened to her, which was a definite blessing. All I knew was that no one was ever going to lay a hand on me against my will. I would never be raped; at least that was the plan.

I was often disturbed by Angel and could not help but pick up on the irony of the work shirt she wore for her job at the Red Roof Inn that simply said, "Sleep Cheap." I did not think very highly of my sister at that time.

LET'S MAKE A DEAL

We left Western's campus and moved to a different neighborhood in the summer of 1976.

I was crushed about moving because this rental property did not allow pets. A few months before the move I found a black cocker spaniel mix on the road that had been hit by a car. I was so excited when Mom and Dad let me keep her. I nursed her back to health, but now we had to move. I named her Whiskey, and I have no idea why, but she was a great source of comfort, and in the end, heartbreak. I remember Dad crying as he loaded Whiskey in the car to take her to the dog pound.

I was off to junior high school. Christopher and Sissy were older now and both had graduated from Hackett Catholic Central High School. They were doing the college thing and were no longer subjected to the wrath of Angel. They were "out of there."

Danny and I walked to school. The first week, I met Tina, a fellow seventh grader, and she invited me to hang out outside the church across the street from school. I was open to making some new friends. This group of punk kids was smoking cigarettes, and Tina gave me one. It was obvious to Tina that I was not a smoker, so as time went on, she taught me how to French-inhale and how to go about blowing smoke rings. She was a pro. Tina could blow a ring through a ring; amazing stuff for a twelve-year-old. I did not hesitate to partake. I wanted to fit in. I was wise enough to make the decision to smoke. I'd grown-up quickly the last couple of years and the timing felt right.

It wasn't long before I walked with a friend to the local Minute Mart, and purchased my first pack of cigarettes—Kool Menthols. I was eleven-years-old, and the cashier didn't even think twice about selling them to me. I switched to Newport, then Marlboro Green, and then finally graduated to Marlboro Reds, nicknamed, "cowboy killers." I smoked Marlboro Reds for thirteen years. I always said, "I'm not a cowboy, so they won't kill me." When I ran out of cigarettes, I even went as far as to roll up butt tobacco. This was great practice for what lay ahead.

Danny made friends with, Mick, an older boy from Tina's neighborhood. The Elmwood neighborhood was quite different from our middle-class neighborhood, but Danny and I ran with the Elmwood Rats just the same. Mick was very handsome, with dark features and long silky black hair. He drove a motorcycle, and I had a major crush on him.

I saw Mick and Danny hanging out in the parking lot of the Third Reformed Church, which was kitty-corner from our home. They were smoking a joint when I walked up, so I joined in—to be cool, of course. It was the first time I willingly smoked dope. I had turned it down at the church next to the school recently, but not this time, not in Mick's presence. I started smoking weed regularly and began dealing drugs only days later. I was not quite twelve-years-old.

Mick was sixteen and a serious drug dealer for his age. Tina lived a few blocks from Mick's house, and we made regular visits to his place to purchase drugs and help him with drug-related tasks, such as, breaking up large quantities of hash that came compressed in tube socks. We weighed out grams on his triple-beam scale and wrapped it in aluminum foil. We bagged quarters, halves, and ounces of weed and tore apart the large sheets of Woodstock and other blotter acid and then helped him get rid of all of it. I bought my first ounce of weed for twenty-five dollars and rolled it into forty joints, which meant, I had fifteen for myself and could sell the rest and get my money back. This was easy to do up at the church before and after school, and so the cycle began.

Mick hung around our house from time to time. We were in the living room one day, and Angel came in and flashed him her breasts and sat on his lap long enough to tease him and me. She was obviously not in her right mind, and enjoying dissing me. Angel was a gorgeous girl, and any boy that met her simply drooled, and she made me feel like dog meat.

I remember, back in the day, my mom talking about how horrible *Playboy* and *Penthouse* were. My mother hated sexploitation of women and wasn't afraid to make her case against the pigs that produced these magazines. As a result, I thought they were disgusting, yet I had a sister that loved to flaunt her stuff. It left scars. I was always threatened by the seductress types. I did not want to be anything like my sister. I preferred to seduce boys with drugs and my bubbly personality.

I really liked Mick and he knew it. He attempted to rape me one night when I got too high and went upstairs to pass out. I was in my bed when he climbed on top of me. I got loud and Mick had no choice but to vacate the premises. Fortunately, he never tried it again. I was not ready for sex. That was a close call.

My life continued toward the darkened realm and I refused to go to church anymore. Mom and Dad were still practicing Catholics. I went to my last couple of youth groups stoned and wasn't getting a thing out of church. I was just going through the motions. I went because that was what we did, no questions asked. I never picked up on the love of Jesus as in Angel's favorite song to sing when we were little, *Jesus Loves Me*. "Jesus loves me, yes I know, for the Bible tells me so…" Yeah, and? I didn't get it. We never studied the Bible at church or at home. Jesus was just the guy that died on a cross; something my dad was into. God had no meaning to me. I guess no one had explained it to me well enough. Dad saying grace at dinner and his artwork were the extent of my exposure to Christianity in our home.

My taste in music changed drastically after I started using drugs. Instead of listening to Sissy's record albums, such as, America, Bread, Cat Stevens and Simon and Garfunkel, I found myself drawn to Angel's music. The first album I remember Angel bringing home was Aerosmith's *Dream On*. Led Zeppelin,

The Rolling Stones, David Bowie, Kansas, and Elton John were some more bands from Angel's early album collection. As I got a little older, I took my listening preference a step further toward the dark and really got into Metallica, Judas Priest, and Black Sabbath to name a few. This music went well with the sick and twisted hallucinogens and dope I was into. I was a thrashing metal, head banger, a burn-out and a stoner.

I was playing with Ouija board's and displayed an upside down cross in my bedroom window.

I suffered from severe acne. It was an extremely humbling affliction, so drugs and alcohol were a way to fit in and self-medicate. I worked hard to make up for my face. Being a dealer was a suitable distraction. I suppose I was not frightening to look at, but I was no natural beauty. Zit coverage was an art that I strived to master. Acne made me feel like a beast.

My appearance began to change drastically, as well; it was that whole peer pressure thing. Green Converse high-tops were the only shoes for me and I had a favorite pair of faded Levis with holes in the knees. I customized them with red bandanas sewn in the butt, leather laced up the sides, and a large "Moby Dick" written in pen on one of the thighs that I retouched after every wash. "Moby Dick," was a Led Zeppelin song with the most amazing drum solo.

I put my hair in multiple braids while it was wet, like Angel did, and when dry, I took them out and had a long kinky mess. I was *too* cool.

Mom took me to get my ears pierced when I was eleven, but the two holes were not enough. A few weeks later, I pierced three more holes in them with a darning needle and an ice cube. I pierced the first one, then skipped the ice for the last two. What's a little pain?

I started skipping school, and my grades began to slip. I earned my first D, and it was the last year I passed an English class. Smoking dope left me with little motivation to go to school.

It was around this time that Mom and Dad allowed me to start smoking cigarettes in the house. They didn't want me to cause a fire by trying to hide it, and honestly, I think Angel had sucked the fight right out of them. They didn't sign up for the challenges Angel presented them and I took advantage of their weakness. Of course, I had my Dad's SAFTI-PLUS ashtray, the best ashtray in the world.

TRIPPED OUT

My love affair with the "almighty buzz" allowed me to block out the harsh reality of my home life. Any extracurricular activities were basically none existent. Left to my own devises, drugs became a sport for me. I had all kinds of paraphernalia, from toke stones and bongs I purchased at the local Boogie Records—again, no questions asked—to the pipes I made from stuff I purchased or stole from the hardware store. Chamber weed from a chamber pipe I made, and generation roach weed was the flavor of the day. Smelly, stinky, sticky resin was the rave. It seemed to be a competition between us stoners.

By the end of summer after seventh grade, I was taking up to three hits of LSD a day. It was a wicked buzz on so many levels. I was very cautious about where I tripped and with whom. I couldn't really say I ever had a bad trip, but the three or four hours it took to come down off the buzz were absolutely horrid. I felt that it was what you made of it though, and it came down to mind control. I found it to be a freaky challenge. Mushrooms were also plentiful and used for trippin'.

I witnessed many kids having very violent reactions on hallucinogens—punching glass and getting into bloody fights. A group of us Elmwood Rats witnessed a mean boy get shot in the leg in broad daylight while we were in the midst of a trip. Big buzz kill. I'm pretty sure Satan is pro LSD and other hallucinogens.

—⁂—

I spent the night at Tina's a lot. It took the pressure off of my mom and dad. They worked fulltime and Angel took the rest of their energy.

Tina and I would trip and get stoned and listen to her folk's Led Zeppelin and Santana albums. We were stealing beers and packs of smokes when we thought we could get away with it; we didn't always, but Tina's parents were cool about it.

We took on a babysitting job just around the corner from her home. Two single moms living together, each with an eight-year-old boy. We thought these women were so awesome, giving us the boys' Ritalin just for the buzz of it. These gals did a bit of dealing themselves, so they also put us to work filling capsules with speed. They rarely paid us any cash for watching the boys; we gladly accepted drugs as payment.

Mom and Dad got me a couple of babysitting jobs, too, but I was completely irresponsible. I stole packs of cigarettes from one place and left a little bottle of roaches in the bathroom at the other. I got stoned after the baby went to sleep. That couple never called me again or notified my parents. Whoosh! I repent as I recall my past. My life had become a long string of dirty deeds, from dealing to stealing to doping and trippin'.

INVISIBLE

We moved again the summer after I finished seventh grade. Dad was in real estate by this time and was doing better financially. He found Mom her dream home in an upscale neighborhood. It was half a mile from our previous home, but it put me in a different junior high for eighth grade. I went with bells on and made a name for myself rather quickly, smoking in the bathroom and selling joints on the steps at lunch. Business was booming; thirty to forty joints went in about twenty minutes daily.

I was officially boy crazy and my dating career did not start out too smoothly. There was a boy I had my eye on who was from out of state. The rumor was that another girl wanted him too. We were destined to fight for him, and we did in the hallway during lunch, with a crowd watching and cheering. It was my first and only fistfight (my brother Danny doesn't count), and I'm not sure if I won the fight, but I won the boy. I lost my virginity to him on Halloween, one week before I turned thirteen. He wound up breaking his leg in the very first football game of the season, and I broke up with him.

My next boyfriend was a *real* football star, but I was growing fond of his best friend, so I broke up with him in hopes of nabbing Joshua. Eventually, Joshua came around, and I took his virginity. We had so much fun hanging out. He was a real good kid, athletic with good grades, not to mention gorgeous.

Six months after we started dating, Joshua's mother suffered a massive stroke; she was thirty-three years old. Joshua cut me off abruptly after that. I was crushed that he would not allow me to comfort him; not even for a day. My head spun and I could not shake it. Getting an education was the last thing on my mind. Overwhelmed with heart break, I made friends with Joshua's cousins, hoping to gain access to him. These three sisters lived only a block from Joshua.

Joshua's mother eventually came home, and she needed constant care, which put a huge burden on this beautiful teenage boy and his older sister. Together with his cousins, I made several visits to Joshua's home, always looking for an opening to get close him and, of course, to spend time with his mother, whom I had grown very fond of. She liked me.

The visits were extremely painful. As Joshua helped his mom around the home, she'd pee on the floor; and as he tried to feed her, she'd spit. She had lost the ability to speak, and she drooled, although, Joshua's big sister did tell me that she still found ways of communicating. She was thirty-nine when she passed away. I suffered a severe broken heart, but my pain was trivial in comparison to what Joshua was forced to deal with. I just wished he would have let me help him somehow. I stayed single for a long time in hopes Joshua would someday return to me. Oh, how I loved that boy.

I started spending a lot of time with Joshua's cousins—Jenny, Judy, and Janice. Most mornings I'd walk to their house. They were tough girls from growing up with their own issues at home. We'd hang out after their dad went to work and get drunk and high. We also spent more time than I liked to admit, watching soap operas.

Jenny was old enough to drive, so their mom let us borrow her car. We cruised the park across the street from the high school, jamming to Nazareth's "Hair of the Dog," one of two eight tracks they owned. This went on for a couple of years, but it never got me any closer to Joshua. My theme song was the ballad "Love Hurts" by Nazareth.

I used artwork as a distraction and an outlet for my broken heart. My art classes were always important to me and I spent a lot of time drawing and doodling on my folders during classes. Some of my classmates took notice of my art, and much to my surprise, kids were offering me money to draw pot leaves, Medusas, and flaming joints on their folders. I was trippin' in pre-algebra one day when my teacher approached my desk while I was busily working on a stack of folders. He asked what I was doing, and I showed him some of my work. He actually complimented me and went back to teaching. I really liked him after that.

I had lost almost all interest in school after Joshua cut me off. I was a goof off in class and I only did what I liked and refused to do what I didn't and received my fair share of detentions. I didn't want to be in school anyway. It was really awkward seeing Joshua in the hallways. He acted as if I were invisible.

HIGH SCHOOL HIGH

By the time I started high school, Angel was around age eighteen and managing to hold down a job, waiting tables at a Greek restaurant in downtown Kalamazoo. She met a man, and they got married. Angel gave birth to her first child just before she turned nineteen. She was a stay-at-home mom, and it seemed to agree with her. Our family was relieved and thankful she had finally cleaned up her act. This baby was her saving grace. Her son was an answer to many prayers. The magnitude of the impact that this child had on my sister was absolutely unbelievable. Angel's life had changed, seemingly, overnight. I knew my mom and my dad were praising God. They endured something that would have ripped most marriages apart. And believe me, I heard the word *divorce* during many heated arguments.

I was now a sophomore at Loy Norrix high school and very happy for Angel's new life. My friends and I spent endless hours playing Frisbee at Milham Park, directly across the street from school. I earned my park ranger certificate by spending more than twenty hours a quarter there. It was given to me by a fellow incorrigible. He made them at school—very authentic looking—with a picture of Smokey the Bear hitting a joint. It was even signed and dated.

By the time I was fourteen, alcohol had become a regular form of entertainment. There were at least a dozen of us who regularly met at a hangout near the liquor store. We'd pool our money and a girlfriend and I would wait in the parking lot until we found a willing buyer. It was so easy. We started out drinking Boones Farm and Mad Dog but quickly graduated to Jim Beam, Jack Daniel's, Seagram's, or Black Velvet with a beer chaser. A pint of Jim Beam with a quart of Miller Genuine Draft was my preference. We partied way too hard.

Two of the young men in my high school group who hit the bottle the hardest became severe alcoholics while still in their teens. Bobby ate the tops off beer bottles and could put his fist through the windshield of a car. He had this thing about punching glass. I took him to the emergency room on two occasions, with his head in my lap, while he was bleeding severely. He wound up getting several DUIs early on and lost his license for many years.

The other boy was a fighter, and smoking-hot. We called him Dr. Jimmy, after the song "Dr. Jimmy and Mr. Jim" by The Who. He was a Jekyll-and-Hyde character. When he started drinking, he became insane. He was a magnet for violence and preferred starting brawls.

These guys barely survived their teens and have both been sober for many years. Dr. Jimmy had Jesus with the thorny crown tattooed on his arm.

I had the same teachers for biology and algebra three years in a row. I knew this stuff forward and backward. I'd show up the day of a test, ace it, and still fail the class because of my absences. It didn't make sense to me. You could call me a rebel.

One art teacher gave me As regardless of my absences. Mr. Smith was a gay black man who thought I had talent and he prominently displayed my art in the hallways. I had a horrible experience with my other art teacher. I was working on a masterpiece, *The Stairway to Heaven*. I'd been working so hard on this drawing. The teacher came to my desk, and all he said was, "I don't like the subject matter. You need to choose something else." I was crushed. I grabbed my things, flipped him the bird, and never returned to his classroom. I went to find Mr. Smith. I was upset and crying when I told him what happened and he gave me a big hug. I showed him the picture, and he said, like only Mr. Smith could say, "Sister, honey, lover, child, that is fabulous!" He had a huge heart, and let me finish my *Stairway to Heaven* in his classroom. He allowed me to come to *all* his classes, whether or not I was on the class list and even allowed me to smoke a cigarette in the room during lunch hour while I worked on my art.

Mom and Dad finally gave me an ultimatum—start going to school and get passing grades or start working. I was fifteen but lied about my age and got my first job at Burger King, although I did continue to attend an ocassional class based on it's importance to me.

The Burger King parking lot happened to be one of my hangouts and was directly across the street from my favorite liquor store and within walking distance from home.

I met my new boyfriend while working at Burger King. John was nineteen and a good old boy, with cowboy boots and a hat, and you rarely saw him without a Mountain Dew in his hand. He drove a sweet bright-yellow car and owned a pickup truck and worked for the City Yards.

He taught me how to drive his Chevy pickup with a three speed on the column, so by the time it came to taking my driver's education class, I'd already driven a couple of thousand miles. I chose the only standard transmission on the lot. I passed that class with flying colors thanks to John's instruction.

Driving made dealing a lot more convenient. I didn't have to rely on my friends or ride the school or city bus to get to the park, where I conducted my business before, during, and after school. My boyfriend trusted me with his beautiful white truck. This was when my dad stopped me one day on my way out the door with a bottle of beer in my hand. He took my beer into the kitchen and poured it into a coffee mug and said, "If you are going to drink and drive, do it incognito." I thanked Dad and jumped in the truck and took off. Hey, if I was going to do it, he wanted me to be smart about it.

I wanted to surprise John by filling up the gas tank before I picked him up from work one afternoon. My very first trip to the gas pumps went really bad. I managed to get the gas all right, but when I pulled out, that stupid red pole creased the entire truck bed. I picked him up from work bawling my head off, figuring he'd kill me, but he just started laughing uncontrollably. It must have been love. My parents loved him, but I broke up with him after about six months. It was time to move on.

The park rangers had a couple of sweet party spots in town. We had huge bonfires made with skids and multiple kegs pretty much every weekend. We had my "sweet sixteen" in one of these spots—several kegs and dozens of kids, the epitome of a teenage wasteland. I was single at the time and laid three boys that night. My mom approached me about birth control when I was fifteen, and I very matter-of-factly told her I'd been on the pill for two years and not to worry.

My next boyfriend while I was "in high school" was my brother Danny's, best friend Steve, an intelligent preppy, or so he appeared. He loved to smoke large quantities of dope, trip, and drink. Danny was upset with my choice of boyfriend, but that didn't stop me. You could call it paybacks for the endless hours of feedback I endured from his electric guitar. Danny's bedroom was located below mine, and he had absolutely no mercy on me. I swear he played it just to annoy me half the time. Steve and I were together for over three years. Just before we started dating, he had been busted for painting graffiti on a church: "Lord, don't strike that poor boy down," lyrics from a Van Halen song. We had a great relationship. We loved trippin' on mushrooms and going to concerts. The Scorpions were our favorite band but we also enjoyed dozens of others. We played tons of Frisbee, hit the beach, and took long rides on his old Triumph motorcycle. Steve and I were inseparable until the day he told me he'd slept with a neighbor girl. That was the end of us. I walked away and never looked back.

My senior year in '83, I dropped out for good. I left high school with a total of nine credits. You needed twenty-one to graduate. Six credits were from ninth grade at the junior high. The other three were, of course, driver's education and art. I went to adult education, and earned my GED a month before my class graduated.

I enrolled in a local community college the next fall and went part-time for a number of years and enjoyed every minute of it. Even though I did not complete all my classes or end up with a degree, I went because I wanted to, not because I had to. I felt that I received more of an education and discipline from working full-time than jumping through hoops in school. I thank my parents for forcing me to work and not making a huge deal out of not being your typical student. My parents had faith in me. I was a hard worker and was responsible at home—keeping my room immaculate, cleaning the house, doing laundry, and even folding Dad's tightie whities and ironing his hankies. I owed my parents. I respected them and did what was necessary to live in harmony with them. If I slipped, Dad would say, "Don't leave that for your mother to do!" His tone was not always pleasant, but that was okay.

HELL-BENT-FOR-LEATHER

I quit my job at Burger King and applied for a job at Dunkin Donuts under the advice of my brother Danny's girlfriend. I got the job and was allowed to work a lot of overtime, frequently up to fifty-five hours a week. I graduated to donut maker after a year or so. I was second-shift baker for three years and I thrived on hard work. I did it all, and the manager loved me. I was very responsible, learned quickly, and quality was a high priority for me.

My manager knew I was a party girl. He often left twelve-packs of beer in my car. When we received the Big One travel mugs for retail sales, he brought one to me while I was working first shift. To my pleasant surprise, it was full of beer. He would keep my mug topped off for me on a daily basis, and I was allowed to get stoned outside, behind the dumpster as long as I was cool about it.

While working one night, an older boy who lived in my neighborhood came in and asked if I'd like to buy some cocaine. I purchased a gram and met him at his house after work. I was eighteen-years-old. I'd been curious about cocaine for a while, and this seemed the perfect opportunity; the natural course of action. I was happy with my life that revolved around partying. I was enjoying my identity of extreme party girl, with no intentions of slowing down.

This boy, my first cocaine connection, was already deep into his addiction. He was sweating profusely as he prepared it. I could tell this was an art, and he was a master. I was intrigued. My very first experience with cocaine was in the smokable form, freebasing—what we call crack today. There was only one right way to cook it, and it was very involved, with numerous steps requiring precision. I learned how to freebase from a pro.

I was hooked that night and chased cocaine for five long years. Having a credit card was problematic. I maxed out the $300 limit with a cash advance the very first time I used it, and bought an eight ball of cocaine to cook up.

I loved freebasing and hit the pipe hard, blacking out on numerous occasions, coming out of it while people stood around me wondering if I was dead. I loved tempting fate; it was in my blood. I'd stand up and do it again and again in search of the ultimate hit; on a quest for the almighty buzz.

Freebasing was very expensive and not always convenient, so I also snorted unthinkable amounts. All I cared about outside of work now was my new best friend. To say that cocaine is alluring was a gross understatement. In the beginning, the feelings of mental clarity, self-confidence, overall well-being and completeness, kept me craving more. This was a revolutionary buzz for me. Everyone needed to try this stuff. I thought I was all that when I was using cocaine, plus I could smoke dope and drink endless amounts as long as I had some to snort. There were frequent three-, four-, or even five-day binges. I'd make it through work by doing lines in the bathroom and would return to the dealer's house where these types of parties never seemed to have an end, and freebase some more.

I snorted too much cocaine a few times and had to go to the doctor's office; my nose so packed with cocaine that I lost my voice. I could not make a peep. As a result of snorting so much I eventually lost the use of my right nostril. There was simply no more suction, when I sniffed, nothing happened. I would snort just about anything else too—Tylox, Percodan, Percocet, Darvon, and let's not forget Methamphetamine. Crush a pill or empty out the capsule, and I had an instant buzz. I enjoyed pills. Really, I enjoyed just about anything mood-altering. No needles, though. I always refused shooting heroin. I was smart enough to know that shooting heroin would be my demise, or to put it more bluntly, I wasn't stupid enough to try it. I'd been around my share of shooters and was not impressed. Surely, Neil Young's song, "Needle and the Damage Done" helped my decision to not go that route, with it's very eerie lyrics. I did have my limits.

I liked to think I was a pool hustler. I frequented a couple of dive bars where I had cocaine connections. One of the bars was only three doors down from the donut shop. Working second shift allowed me to close the bar most nights. I was a decent shooter and played for ten bucks, or sometimes for beers. I knew the bouncers well, so if I had a problem with a guy not paying me, I'd go tell my buddy at the door. That usually solved my problem. You'd be surprised how many guys tried to stiff me. I was pretty serious and carried baby powder in my purse, just in case the bars didn't have any.

I must have thought I was having fun. I kept getting deeper and deeper into the chasm of the lost. No one in their right mind would find my lifestyle acceptable. It was only for the perverted and twisted soul.

I took major risks for the sake of a buzz. Many more times than I'd like to admit when I was hooked on cocaine. My party buddies were primarily males. Most girls couldn't begin to keep up with me. I didn't hang around people that might slow me down.

My risky business led to rape. The fact was I lost count of the number of times I had sex under duress and scared out of my mind. Call it a survival instinct, but as frightening and degrading as it was, I felt that putting out was the safest thing to do most times.

If I thought I could get out, I would. I fought my way out one time after being thrown on the bed. I thought we were going to do some lines but this creep proceeded to maul me. I went ballistic and he backed off just enough, and I made my escape. I left his home with no coat or shoes in the middle of winter. This was one of the scariest moments of my life. I went to the donut shop, a few blocks away and my manager was working so I cried on his shoulder for a little bit, pulled myself together, and drove home with only a shred of dignity.

I never thought twice about drinking and driving and any car was a party mobile to me.

I rolled my dad's car in a blizzard when I was nineteen, beyond wasted. Joshua's cousin, Judy, and I went to my favorite club for picking up bass players. It was Free Champagne Night for Ladies that Friday, and a snow storm would not stop me. Heaven forbid I miss this night. I had drugs to sell at the club in my usual style. The club was said to be owned by the Mob, and it was the one place where minors could easily get away with drinking.

We left near closing time to head home. I fired up a joint and we were jamming to Judas Priest's "Hell-Bent-for-Leather." I made a wrong turn, and we headed down a country road, snow-blind and driving too fast for the conditions. We spun out, clipped a telephone pole in half, took out a speed limit sign, rolled three times, and ended up in a celery patch.

The base of the telephone pole was sticking out of the snow a couple of feet, and the rest of the pole was still hanging by the wires, stuck in the snow a few feet away. I was driving Dad's four-door Pontiac Phoenix. The pole hit between the two doors on my side. There were only a few inches left between my seat and the steering wheel and I was told that if I had been wearing my seat belt, I would have been crushed to death. Mom and Dad had always encouraged me to wear my seat belt, and I did for the most part, but not this night!

I was thrown into my friend. The force of my body hitting hers broke both bones in her left arm and ejected her into the snow. She went into shock after she saw me hanging out of the passenger door looking good and dead. I don't remember anything until I woke up in an ambulance. Someone driving a truck in front of us saw us go off the road and summoned help. It was a small miracle anyone was out and about due to the weather conditions. I woke up screaming bloody murder. I was strapped down and was demanding that the EMT turn me over because my back was broken. I kept passing out from the intense pain.

The cops were at the hospital when the ambulance arrived and they refused to let the nurse take a blood alcohol test; it must have been a Mob thing. Rumor was the cops that patrolled that area were paid off. Let's face it, drunken driving busts of underage individuals in close vicinity to the bar might send up red flags, and that would be bad for a booming business. I received a forty-dollar ticket for driving too fast for the dangerous conditions. Case closed.

Judy's sister's, Jenny and Janice, made it to the scene of the accident early the morning after and recovered my purse with the baggy of joints and the speeders I had for sale that night. I was very thankful to them.

I had a concussion, numerous abrasions and bruises on the left side of my body, three broken ribs, and punctured lungs. Broken ribs must be the worst. I couldn't cough, sneeze, laugh, or go to the bathroom without severe pain. The first thing I did when I got to my hospital room was ask for my smokes. I had to take very shallow puffs due to the fluid in my lungs. This clearly speaks to the addictive qualities of cigarettes.

During my first few weeks at home, I found my water bed impossible to sleep on, so instead, I camped out on the couch in the family room with my rib brace, dope, beer, and pain pills. My parents were just happy I was alive. I don't think the thought ever crossed their mind that I might be overindulging. I was just me being me.

I am embarrassed to share that only two months after this horrible accident, I totaled vehicle number two.

I begged and begged my dad to borrow the car just this once. I had been cut off from the family vehicles. Dad told me after the last accident not to ever ask to drive his car again, but this was a special occasion. I had a hair appointment and my ride canceled on me, and Dad gave in.

Before the appointment I grabbed an ice tea at the McDonald's drive-thru. As I was leaving and attempting to make a left turn, I was broad sided by a speeding car. At least that was my story. We both got a ticket.

This was the most difficult phone call that I had ever made. I informed poor Dad that I wrecked another one of his vehicles. I never did make it to my hair appointment. There was, of course, no alcohol involved in this accident. I was drinking ice tea. I was stoned but that went undetected, and the cop never checked my purse where he would have found a variety of drugs and paraphernalia.

I caused my parents enough pain and financial burden from the auto accidents and medical bills. I decided it was time to try and make it on my own.

I moved in with a girlfriend from work. She was a single mom and fellow baker. We worked opposite shifts, so I could babysit and help with the rent and finally be independent. She lived in a house in a small town about twenty miles away. One night, I was home alone with a bunch of cocaine and snorted the whole pile. Not an easy task, but I couldn't stop until it was gone. I was totally out of control. What a horrible thing chasing the initial feeling and never being able to achieve it again. But I almost died trying more than once. My girlfriend found me in a lump on her couch and notified my parents. I was down and out and could barely move. Mom took me to the doctor who gave me two choices: blood transfusion or three weeks of bed rest. I was incredibly anemic. I chose bed rest and moved back to Mom and Dad's; so much for my independence.

I never told my mom or the doctor how I got in that condition. The questions were never asked and I did not divulge my dirty little secret. As far as they knew I was just not feeling well. I had no intentions of giving up cocaine or my lifestyle. I continued to deny that how I was living was horribly wrong. I had no concept of what may be considered unacceptable to the average person. As long as I wasn't hurting anyone I felt it only right that I be left to my own devises. Hey, it was *my* life. Intervention was the last thing I wanted.

I still had my job at the donut shop. There was a new hire, Ian, and he was a real cutie. Ian was from a local halfway house where my manager often recruited young men to mop floors and clean. This young man had been in trouble with the law and had an impressive record for a seventeen-year-old: three breaking and entering and two grand car auto thefts. I was attracted to him, and I introduced him to cocaine, and we quickly became an item.

After being released from the halfway house, Ian moved in with Peter, a Vietnam veteran who was in a desperate state. Peter was a decorated veteran and was living alone at the mercy of his wife and children who had turned on him. They took everything but his bed and a sofa. He did not have an appliance to prepare a meal if he could. This tortured soul was but a stump of a man—legless, lacking an arm, and blind. Disgraced by the treatment from his wife and children, Ian and I asked my parents to help this poor veteran, so they hired their attorney to work on severing his relationship with his wife. His own family was attempting to ruin him financially and otherwise. I could not understand his wife's hatred toward him. She barged in the front door one day and threw a bag of cut-up credit cards at him, announcing that she had maxed them all out, cursing all the while.

Peter hit the bottle hard and abused any drug he could get his hands on, including his prescriptions, oftentimes falling out of his wheelchair and unable to get back in without assistance. Ian and I had the unfortunate experience of discovering him dead one evening, lying on his sofa in just his underwear, with an empty pill bottle nearby. What I witnessed in those few months was a crude example of what should not happen to a wounded war hero. Ian and I did all we could to help, but we were too late. We attended Peter's funeral, and one of his children had the nerve to come over and accuse us of his demise. This was one of the creepiest experiences of my life. Why did life have to be so cruel sometimes? I went into numb mode, and my relationship with Ian fell apart; I was so self-absorbed in my sorrow and addictions.

I continued to run like a hamster on a wheel, and I started using more meth for added stamina. Plus, it didn't disappear as fast as the cocaine. I was equally addicted to both and already an alcoholic. When I got high, I had to drink; and when I started to drink, I had to have lines. I would not stop until I found what I needed. Luckily, I had a large number of connections.

Strip clubs were one of the easiest places to find stuff when I was getting desperate. I was the kind of girl who could belly up to a bar anywhere, all alone, and have the time of my life. The strip club owners loved to see me walk into their establishments, always recruiting me for amateur nights, tempting me with drinks, T-shirts, coasters, and whatever. Nothing worked. You couldn't pay me enough to disrespect myself that way. I always felt sorry for those girls.

I was still on a roll and for my twenty-first birthday, I pulled out the big guns—a case of beer, half an ounce of weed, and an eight ball of coke (three-and-a-half grams), with three hits of orange sunshine (acid) chopped up into it. I almost lost it that night when I had to take my girlfriend from the donut shop home to her small town. I started hallucinating on the highway and was forced to pull over. We sat there for hours. I smoked some more dope, trying to take the edge off. It was a long-term deal.

SO SUE ME

I was twenty-one years old, with adult size problems and a pea sized brain, apparently. My poor decisions had the potential for much greater repercussion, and something was always happening to keep me on my toes. I slept right through many "wake-up calls."

A lawsuit was brought against me by a local motel. This was quite a surprise. The thought never crossed my mind that my attempt to avoid harm could have any repercussions.

I went to pick up a bag of weed and met a guy there who needed a ride someplace. I agreed to take him, but what he really wanted was me. He was freaking me out because he kept insisting we get a room. I pulled up to this seedy motel, but when he wanted me to go in and pay for a room, I refused and gave him my credit card. I burned rubber as soon as he stepped out of my very speedy '78 Pontiac Trans Am, Smoky and the Bandit–style, red, with the black-and-gold bird on the hood.

The room was in my name, of course, and he trashed the place, broke the furniture, smashed the mirrors, and punched holes in the walls. I felt lucky to be alive, or at least not raped. The motel tried to sue me for damages. Come to find out, you can't get blood out of a turnip. Two weeks later, Mom saw in the newspaper that this creep was in jail for a stabbing. I did the right thing; no regrets there.

Another example would be when I very nearly killed a man. My girlfriend from the donut shop and I were at a dive bar after hours. They locked the door and let us stay; this was typical. I was shooting pool and this biker dude took a liking to me. My girlfriend was with her boyfriend. The four of us decided to grab some breakfast. Hey, maybe this would go somewhere. He was good-looking, polite, had a decent job, and drove a Harley. What more could I ask for?

I got in my car and rolled down my window to say, "See you there." I watched him walk around the other side of the car and put on his helmet. Sweet! I put my car in reverse and nailed it like you do in a '78 Trans Am. It seems as though he had something urgent to tell me that couldn't wait until we got to the restaurant. I felt this *thump*, *thump* and saw him slam into a parked truck behind me. Yep, I backed right over him and he wouldn't let me take him to the hospital. He still wanted to have breakfast with me so he climbed in my car.

We got him to our table at the restaurant, propped up his injured ankle, and watched it swell—not a pretty sight. He wound up going to the doctor later that morning, and his ankle was destroyed. He would have pins in it for the rest of his life. Get this—he still wanted to date me. I just couldn't after that. I don't think we got off on the right foot.

He tried to sue me, but didn't get anywhere. He should have gone to the emergency room right away and immediately filed a police report. This was another close call.

ESCAPE FROM THE ZOO

My manager at Dunkin' Donuts was now the owner. Still very fond of me, he gave me a huge raise when he took over. He was an older man, married with children, and suffered from rosacea. Alcoholism was written all over his face.

He started hanging around a lot more than normal and inviting himself to the bar with me after work. I used to think he was okay, but he was really starting to give me the shivers. He was coming in intoxicated and whispering disgusting things in my ear in the back room, or even while I was up front serving customers—sexual harassment, no doubt. The final straw happened when he goosed me good while behind the coffee counter, in front of a bunch of regulars. He was wasted out of his mind and laughing hysterically while I walked out the door in the middle of my shift, never to return. Not long after I quit the donut shop he was busted for embezzling and it went down the tubes.

It was a gut-wrenching experience, but I quickly found employment at Meijer Thrifty Acres, working in health and beauty aids and the pharmacy. I was filling prescriptions and stealing Xanax from the automatic dispenser. Xanax was not a highly controlled substance; the real good stuff was under lock and key.

I met a young man from another department that had a connection to pain pills. They were cheaper than cocaine, and when added to alcohol it was a respectable buzz.

His buddy had an out-of-town pharmacist that wrote him dirty prescriptions. We spent our time together drinking and snorting and/or popping pills. It was about three months after I met this guy with the pharmacist connection, that he was found leaning up against a tree dead in front of his apartment on a very busy road in downtown Kalamazoo, overdosed on pain meds.

Clearly, I didn't know what end was up. I was doing any drug I could get my hands on and was struggling with credit card debt and was no longer able to keep up with my bills. The cocaine finally took its toll on my finances. I sold my waterbed, sweet Marantz stereo, and Trans Am, all for the sake of the almighty buzz.

I eventually confessed to my parents that I was a cocaine addict, and how I'd gotten myself into a financial mess. There was no talk of counseling or rehabilitation. That wasn't the kind of help I was looking for. To look at me, you would never suspect I'd done any drugs. I was working steady and still kept up with my chores at home, so not needing outside help was an easy sell. I only wanted help getting out of my financial rut. I handed over my paycheck every week and Mom put me on a strict budget.

I fully understood now how the homeless addict could lose all desire for anything that resembled normal. For the addict, it was almost impossible to see beyond the next swig or the next hit. It was real and it was frightening.

Tragically, this period of my life included regular visits to the plasma clinic for donations. The facility, conveniently located in the heart of crack town, was surrounded by down on their luck junkies, addicts, and alcoholics. I received about $17 per visit and could only donate every ten days or so, as I recall, and it felt like it took an eternity for the donation process. I hated going there, but I did what I had to do to maintain some type of high. My appetite for cocaine and meth was insatiable.

It was sad to think about the times I spent groveling, picking through the carpet, hoping to find a misplaced rock or, for heaven's sake, a roach. In those days it was not so much what to get buzzed on, but to achieve a buzz of any kind; anything to distract from the devastating withdrawal symptoms of the last big binge. So no matter how hard I tried, I continued *jonesing* (a craving related to chemical dependence) for the hardcore druggables. It was an inexplicably depressing and irritable feeling.

I was twenty-two years old and obviously, was in desperate need for a change of scenery. My sister Sissy was married and living in Iowa. She was pregnant with her first child and running their flower shop while her husband was busy working their landscape and lawn service. I asked if I could come down and work for her. I explained my reasons. She too was in desperate need of help and support. The plan was for me to stay for six months—three months before she gave birth to learn the flower business and three months after to run it. My goal was to get away from the cocaine and meth. I didn't even take any weed with me. Alcohol and cigarettes would have to suffice. I figured it would be easy in this small town, population of 450. How much trouble could I get into there?

It was literally a one-stop town, and when I arrived, a cop pulled me over. He had been expecting me. *Oh snap, what did I get myself into?*

I started work right way, and after my first day at the flower shop, I decided to check out the only bar in town, conveniently located directly across the street from my new place of employment.

I was bellied up to the bar at my new watering hole, not long after arriving in town and was craving a buzz. I asked the guy next to me if he knew where I could find some weed. To my surprise, he said he was a cop. No harm done. At least I knew the other cop in town now.

I did not receive a warm welcome from my brother-in-law, Richard. It was obvious that I was a stressor to their relationship. The fact that I drank was a huge problem for Richard. We did not see eye-to-eye on anything, but I could tell how much Sissy really needed my emotional support, along with help at the flower shop.

Sissy was married to a miserable soul. In her early adult life, Sissy wanted to be a nun but instead married a man who used scripture as a means to beat her down and control her. I could see right through him, and I think he knew it.

Richard tried to control me the best he could. I ran the flower business by day and worked with him by night, landscaping, hauling bark, painting the barn, you name it. When I did have the opportunity to make it to the bar, I was raring to go.

The night before Sissy gave birth; I was hanging out at the Lions Clubs in town with a fine corn fed boy, who was my dope connection, as well as lover. We were drinking screwdrivers. The hard stuff always had a way of biting me in the butt. Richard woke me up not long after I came home and passed out. He told me to go change the sign on the highway to read, "It's a Boy!" I was in very bad shape and changed the sign in-between puking episodes. I opened the flower shop that morning. The phone was ringing off the hook; flower orders for Sissy, plus I had funeral arrangements to do that day. I hung out in the large cooler where the cut flowers were kept as much as possible and had a garbage can next to the table for flower arranging. I wish I could have slept it off. This was the longest day of life.

I begged to leave after four months, but Sissy refused to let me go. I had to move out just to finish my sentence. Sissy introduced me to a respectable older gentleman who lived in a nearby town. I rented a room from him the last two months I lived in Iowa, but I was still under Richard's thumb, and he continued to press down hard.

The gentleman who took me in had a son who went to the University of Nebraska. He came home most weekends, and I now had a cocaine connection. He was a real cool kid. We enjoyed listening to Jethro Tull together. Our favorite song was "Skating Away," as the lyrics go, "On the thin ice of new day." That was about right. Let's just say he made the rest of my stay bearable. I completed my sentence, leaving Sissy to suffer all alone. I made the fifteen-hour drive home in twelve, stopping only twice to hit the restroom, listening to the only cassettes I had with me—Metallica's *Master of Puppets*, Steely Dan's *Gold*, and Jackson Browne's *Running on Empty*.

I was back in the "Zoo," and it felt great to be home, but I didn't want to hang out with the old crowd, so I found a job outside of town, at a plastics plant, working second shift, of course. I was doing my best to refrain from the hard core druggables. Pot and alcohol were not the issue. I had absolutely no intention of ever giving *those* up.

I went to the Hash Bash in Ann Arbor and purchased my first "Dugout," which I preferred to call a "one-y." This revolutionized my dope-smoking habit—pack weed in the end and take a hit—hence my nickname: the one-y. I could get stoned virtually anywhere with very little residual smoke. I didn't have to interrupt my fun and leave the bar to get high anymore, if I was slick about it—and I was. When I was a kid I smoked large quantities, up to an ounce a week. I still smogged often, but the one-y allowed me to have a more consistent buzz and a "wake and bake" set the mood for the day; what I called an attitude adjustment. Not being stoned was not normal for me. I hid it incredibly well and that's how I functioned. I was a professional drug and alcohol user and abuser. I was twenty-three and continued to perfect my career. At the very least, it was a serious hobby.

SHATTERED

My new job in plastics was going great —running presses and trimming parts. Quality Control loved me. I was all about quality. I thought of trimming plastic as an art. This prototype shop ran production on aluminum molds, so the amount of flash (excess plastic) could be overwhelming. I'd get my pattern down and out-trim the best of them. I was a trimming fool.

I made friends with the other dope smokers as we indulged on breaks. One guy, who was a flirt and, to my, not so pleasant surprise, into cocaine, invited me to do a line in his car; he was a toolmaker and a married man. We started having sex in his car after work, which led to closing the local bar most nights and going to the hot tubs after work. It all came to an abrupt end when he totaled his truck after a hot tub romp. He missed several days of work. I wasn't sure what happened. I didn't have his phone number. We never called each other. He returned to work humbled. He had confessed to his wife, and that gig was over. Frankly, I was just happy he was alive.

So, I set my sights on a boy named Timothy, who was a troubleshooter/mold setter at the plastics plant. He was a brilliant kid, four years younger than me; 6'4", slim, with gorgeous hazel eyes. He was sweet and shy, and did I mention he was super smart? He was waiting for an opening in the tool department and had plans of becoming a mold maker. Timothy was a straitlaced country boy, the youngest of seven, and was raised a Catholic. I admired the fact that he had never done drugs. That was hard for me to imagine. I fell in love with his combination of innocence and brilliance. We started dating and married about eight months later, on December 1, 1990. I was twenty-five years old and my need for the hard core drugs simply vanished. Love was a powerful thing.

Timothy and I planned on being married forever. Didn't everyone? Our parents were great role models, neither having been divorced. We were meant to be together for better or for worse, so the saying goes.

We were living in an apartment, saving money for a down payment on a house and working on making babies. I wanted five boys! The thought of having girls frightened me.

Shortly after we married, Timothy had a grand mal seizure on the shop floor. I was there to take him to the hospital. He was diagnosed with epilepsy, and the doctor prescribed him Librium, an anti-seizure medicine and all was well.

I found a better paying job with a wholesale printer while Timothy was getting into tool and die. I was still smoking pot and drinking on a daily basis and exposed Timothy to my vices. He didn't mind if I partied, but it wasn't his thing. He preferred to spend his downtime building and flying radio-controlled aircraft. He was kind of obsessed with it. They were fun to fly, and he *let me* crash a couple. We were getting along great.

I decided to quit my job at the print shop after two years to pursue a career in real estate. My dad was still in the business, and we planned to work together as a father-daughter team. Timothy and I moved into my parents' home with the plan of saving even more money to buy a house after I earned my real estate license.

I started working with Dad in August of '93. Dad was the best mentor ever and absolutely gifted in dealing with people. We made an awesome team with my brains and his good looks, or maybe it was the other way around. Dad was my rock and my biggest fan!

Timothy and I were approaching our third anniversary when unusual things started happening, although I didn't think much about it at the time; hindsight's 20/20. We went to see the movie *The Doors* and Timothy got up and walked out after about twenty minutes. I thought, *Okay, the drug thing turned him off—no biggy.* A few months later, we took a train to Toronto to watch the Tigers play the Blue Jays in the SkyDome from the Hard Rock Café. Sweet! I was in seventh heaven, enjoying the game and my beers, and he walked out right in the middle of it with no explanation. Timothy was becoming strangely despondent.

In October, Timothy came home from work early one day. He was frantically rummaging around in the recreation room where we kept his model plane stuff, and he was mumbling. He would not look at me or respond to my question of why he was home. It was very odd for either one of us to ever miss a day. He was very confused. Nothing that eventually came out of his mouth was making any sense. I never did get a straight answer out of him. He found a pad of paper and started writing nonstop, and the things he wrote were terrifying: "death to my family," "throwing us all off a bridge into a bloody river," and things of that nature.

He was ranting and raving about something whenever I approached him. For instance, he found my lighter and freaked out and threw it in the garbage, while he explained to me that someone could start a fire with it. A minute later, he was hysterical and screaming because somebody threw out a perfectly good lighter.

And then there was the time I had a magazine on the kitchen table open to no particular page. Timothy shoved it in my face, accusing me of trying to tell him something then took off in our five-speed car, and I could hear him jamming the gears as he drove around and around the block. This was in the wee hours of the morning.

He even shredded my *American Poet* poster of Jim Morrison that was hanging on our bedroom wall.

He threatened my life one minute and asked if we could take a walk the next. We *did* go on one walk, and he wanted to knock on everybody's door to meet them, and he thought the dogs we saw that day were talking to him.

I called the police in fear for my life, but they said they could do nothing unless he hurt me first.

Neither one of us barely slept a wink for a two-week period as a continual flood of tears ran down my face.

Mom and Dad were on vacation, so I called Timothy's parents. I was pretty hysterical myself at this point. I began cursing like a sailor at Timothy's dad demanding he come a get his son immediately. I lost it and could not deal with him anymore. I was so scared and so tired that I could feel my brain turning to mush. His father inquired about what he was doing, so I gave him a couple of examples. I could *not* believe the words that came out of my Father-in-law's mouth. He said, "That sounds just like his older brother. He has been in and out of the state hospital for the last ten years. He's a paranoid schizophrenic!" *Okay, well, that explains a lot.*

His parents called the mental health unit and came to my rescue. We had a very difficult time tricking Timothy into taking a drive. Believe it or not, he was very paranoid. We took him in for an evaluation. First, the doctor met with me alone and then with Timothy. The doctor brought me back in, and Timothy made a run for it. I watched from a window as he was tackled, put into a straightjacket, and escorted into the main hospital while I held the commitment papers in my hands. I signed the forms and made the long walk across the parking lot and up to the third floor, where he would spend the next three weeks.

He was quickly diagnosed as bipolar and paranoid schizophrenic. Oddly enough, the song "Lithium" by Nirvana, which Timothy began taking, was very popular at the time. "I love you. I'm not gonna crack." Yes, Timothy was very confused and it was scary.

I met with a therapist in the mental ward on three occasions. He educated me on Timothy's condition and the bleak reality of a long-term relationship with him and his concerns for me. It was unrealistic for me to think we would ever be normal again. The tendency of such persons was to stop taking their meds when they were feeling better. I would spend the rest of my life policing my husband. I knew I could never look at him the same way, as much as I loved him, the thought of having any intimate contact with him was out of the question.

I filed for divorce three weeks after having Timothy committed and told him how sorry I was. Five months later, we held hands in divorce court. He reassured me it was not my fault and he didn't blame me for anything. I never saw him again.

During the course of the five months leading up to our divorce, my world had been rocked hard. I didn't know which end was up. My average weight since my high school years was 127 lbs. It wasn't long after committing Timothy that I dropped down to 110 lbs., very thin by my standards. I was in a severe numbing mode, drowning myself in alcohol and smogging down. Depression had set in, and all I could do was self-medicate. I eventually turned to food as well, and my weight skyrocketed to 155 lbs. in no time.

The weight gain on top of losing the love of my life left me questioning, "Why did this happen to me?" I always believed everything happened for a reason and tried to make the best of a bad situation. I told myself I would not let anything destroy me, but no matter how I tried to look at it, let's face it—I was broken, shattered into little pieces.

The guilt of leaving Timothy was eating me alive even though I knew in my heart that I had made the right decision. I was eventually able to put a positive spin on the tragic ending of my first marriage. Timothy was an angel, my functional savior, sent to rescue me from the deep pit of my hard core addiction to cocaine and meth. All I could do was label him a stepping-stone; chalk it up to just another learning experience. I had to move on and have faith that I would make a full recovery.

I saw an advertisement for a book on the television: *Dianetics*, by L. Ron Hubbard, and I ordered it. I was intrigued and I thought this book could help fill the void I'd been feeling in my life. I read it and it pushed attending retreats, to gain knowledge and I debated for some time about signing up for one. It was tempting. I decided to ask my father's opinion and he gave it to me. He told me Dianetics was garbage, and to leave it alone, so I did.

———

I went back to focusing on real estate. Dad had introduced me to a young girl who was new to real estate as well. She was a newlywed and a funny girl. We hit it off even though she was eight years younger. I also met a pregnant woman that same day who was working in the "dungeon" with the new agents and low producers. She was eight years older than me. These two women became great friends of mine. Lauren, the newlywed, was the force behind my next three relationships. Where would my life be without her? Roxy, headed for her third divorce and pregnant at the time, was very kind to me and opened up about her sordid past. I liked her regardless. I mean, hell, who was

I to judge? I understood that nobody was perfect. I had a high tolerance for people's shortfalls. You see, I had this plank in my eye! Having my new friends, Lauren and Roxy, helped me get back on track. They took the place of therapy. I started to lose the extra weight and was trying to feel human again. I was twenty-eight and single.

JOY AND MERCY

When I was married to Timothy and working at the whole-sale print shop I made some new friends. Sabrina was a typesetter, and Joy was a key-liner. We sometimes hung out at our apartment after work, drinking and getting stoned. We loved to watch *Ren & Stimpy* and *David Letterman*.

Joy was a very frail girl with long black hair and pale skin, which was covered with craters, acne, and large boils. Her hair was draped over her face whenever possible. She wore strictly black and gray and lived alone in a small flea-infested apartment with her cats. Outside of work, she spent most of her time alone, creating works of art to sell at local art shows.

Joy's art was an outlet for her inner turmoil. She had been severely sexually abused by both her mom and her dad when she was a child. Her parents were in and out of mental institutions, and they both committed suicide when she was fifteen. Joy was never able to enjoy a sex life, due to the damage her parents had done. She regularly went to the doctor to have large lesions lanced and drained in her vaginal canal.

I tried to help Joy in any way I could, whether it was buying her a new microwave, a new tire for her old beater, or purchasing her artwork so she could make her rent. Sabrina and I knew Joy was not long for this world. She told us she'd rather be dead than keep living with the memories and constant reminders of the abuse. Three days later, Joy did the deed. Her death was ruled an accident, but Sabrina and I knew better. Cloaked in black late at night, Joy walked in front of a fast-moving car and was pronounced dead at the scene.

Few would ever have such a profound effect on my life. Joy was a constant reminder of how blessed I was. My childhood was a cake walk compared to hers and countless others. If there was a God, why would he allow such things to happen; where was his mercy?

Joy was twenty-seven years old when she passed away. I don't think I could have lasted that long.

Sabrina's boyfriend wrote this poem for her funeral, which only a few attended:

> In desperate hope we go and search for you
> in all the corners of the earth; we find you not.
> Our world is small and what once had graced it
> can never be regained.
> But infinite is your mansion, dear god,
> and seeking her we one day will come to her door.
> We'll stand under the golden canopy of
> the evening sky and lift our eager eyes
> to your face—never to be lost again.
> Until that day, Joy, rest in sunlit gardens
> painting beautiful memories
> on the canvas of our hearts…
> You are truly loved and missed.

I am saddened to say this young poet and musician died of an overdose of pain meds. After Joy's death, I spent four days of solid binge drinking on the sofa in my living room, paralyzed with pain.

SIN CITY

Mom and Dad enjoyed going to Las Vegas and Dad spent extended periods of time there marketing his safety ashtray. The Holiday Inn and Sands Casinos were customers, and Dad always hoped for more. Mom and Dad offered to take me and show me around after the divorce was final.

I loved playing blackjack and the free drinks were a definite bonus. The first time I played was in Atlantic City at Trump Plaza Hotel and Casino. I was clueless how to play, but Dad staked me forty dollars. I didn't listen to his advice and quickly lost. You just hit until you get twenty-one, right? Certainly not the case as I found out after Dad educated me with the basic strategy and gave me a couple books to study. I had the strategy memorized in no time.

I was considering becoming a blackjack dealer in Las Vegas, and on our trip we visited a total of thirty-six casinos. I spoke to many pit bosses, and every single one said I should be a cocktail waitress because they made more money. I had no desire to be pawed and ogled by strange men. For some reason, I already attracted attention without being dressed scantily. That was the last thing I needed. After getting a feel for the atmosphere I came to the conclusion that Vegas would eat me alive. The appeal of the hard core drugs in that environment would be more than I could bear.

I had an amazing experience at Binion's Horse Shoe Hotel and Casino during this trip, while playing blackjack. I was on third base (the seat on the far left when facing the dealer), my favorite spot, playing a dollar game. I had a twenty-dollar stake and was up to about a hundred dollars. The entire table was winning, and the dealer was overpaying me. Dad told me that would happen sometimes if the dealer liked you and to not say a word.

Three fighter pilots at the table started placing money for *me* to bet. They were in Vegas visiting Nellis Air Force Base and enjoying their down time. We had a major trend going at that table, and I was up to $420. Mom and Dad were ready to leave but the pilots insisted I stay and roll the dice for them at the craps table. They promised to take me to our hotel whenever I wanted to go home. Mom and Dad left at two a.m. and I stayed and rolled some dice. One of the guys won an additional six hundred dollars on the craps table, and they called it a night. A limousine picked us up in front of Binion's. They asked for my address so they could send me a little something and dropped me off. These guys were all married with children, and were total gentlemen. We just clicked that night. A couple of weeks after my return home, a package arrived. The letter read:

70th Fighter Squadron "White Knights"

Amy,

Enjoyed the gambling, this is a little something to remember the boys who protect you while you sleep (when we are not at Binion's)! Wear it in good health.

                        Bucky and Dinger

Enclosed was a ball cap with "70th Fighter Squadron, White Knights," and a jet on the front and "Amy" embroidered on the back. How sweet, and the comment about good health was related to my smoking, no doubt. That was the last I heard from them.

THE HAUNTING

Back to reality in the Zoo, Lauren and I were switching shifts for phone duty at the real estate office. There was a walk-in prospect that I begged her to take. She refused, so I reluctantly went to the lobby, feeling fat and zitty as usual in those days. Turned out it was an attractive young man named Tom, who was a first-time home buyer. He hired me on the spot, and we got busy.

We lost out on the first two houses due to multiple offers. It was very difficult to convince him to offer full price because of the competitive seller's market. This was in 1994, around the time the banks started lightening up on their lending practices. Tom learned the hard way.

After finally taking my advice, Tom closed on his first home. We had been working together for a couple of months and fell in lust during the process. I moved in with him when he closed. You could call it a rebound. My divorce had been final only a few months.

We were engaged after about a year and trying to make a baby. I had not been on birth control pills since my marriage, and Timothy and I had been actively trying to make a baby for three years. Thankfully, we never did conceive.

Tom and I were on our way to Cedar Point Amusement Park in Ohio for a fun-filled weekend with a cooler full of beer. On the way, I began having severe pain in my lower abdomen. I thought it may be a bad case of gas or something, but the pain increased, and I started throwing-up in the car, so we bypassed Cedar Point and went directly to the hotel. Tom carried me to our room and tucked me into bed. I was in denial that anything was seriously wrong and choked down another beer.

I passed out from the pain late that afternoon and came out of it around midnight, screaming at the top of my lungs, "Call an ambulance. I'm going to die!" I asked the EMTs, while being treated in the ambulance, if I was going to be okay. This wonderful man reassured me I was going to make it, but my blood pressure was 60/40, an indication of severe internal bleeding, and I was lucky we called when we did.

It took over two hours for them to figure out what was wrong, and during that time, they refused me any pain meds. A doctor finally came in and told me that I was pregnant. I was thrilled and asked if the baby was going to be okay. It was then I learned about ectopic pregnancies. He said the baby was in my tube and could not live, and I was very fortunate to have survived. I went into surgery at four a.m. They did a laparoscopy through my belly button and then cut through my lower abdomen to remove my left tube, which had burst, and part of my left ovary, where they found a cyst.

I had just about every sexually transmitted disease (STD) imaginable over the course of the years—fortunately, nothing untreatable. Prior to my marriage, I was warned by the ob-gyn that the chances of me carrying a baby full term would be slim. I had biopsies, freezings, and laser treatment after the discovery of precancerous cells on my cervix too many times. But what I was not aware of, and abruptly learned, was that the STDs were very likely to have caused the scar tissue in my fallopian tube and blocked the baby's safe passage to my womb. I believe I lost my number one son that day.

I was twenty-nine years old, and my hopes of ever having children were fading fast. I had a lot of unprotected sex in the last five years with one pregnancy that almost killed me, and *did* kill my baby. That was a hard pill to swallow. My past was haunting me. Back to binge drinking. Numb, numb, numb, numb, numb.

Trying hard to recover from our devastating loss, Tom and I took a vacation to Cancun. When we arrived, our room wasn't available yet, so we decided to go poolside, and guess who was there? Junior and Scotty, my favorite bartenders from one of my watering holes! I'd been spending a lot of time bellied up to their bar as of late. They were coppin' some rays. We had Tom take a picture of the three of us poolside, and they kept the photograph pinned up behind the bar for the remainder of their employment at the bar. They were also kind enough to slip me the little bit of weed they had left because they were leaving Cancun that day. What a small world!

Speaking of weed, it just so happened I was also able to score more while we were on an excursion to the Isla Mujeres, off the coast of Cancun. I was pleased to find a shop that sold paraphernalia. I showed the guy working there a pipe and asked if he knew where I could find something to put in it. We spoke the universal language of drugs. He told me to go to a store around the corner in ten minutes, and there would be a bag under a stack of T-shirts. I gave him ten dollars, went around the corner, and scored. I was definitely a fiend.

Tom and I stayed together for a couple more years after losing the baby, but inevitably, we said our goodbyes. No hard feelings. I moved back to Mom and Dad's, which wasn't so bad. By this time, they had put a second kitchen in the basement, and I was able to use a side entrance that was less intrusive.

Real estate was so unpredictable and I was having trouble earning a steady income, and that's what I needed if I was going to make it on my own. Getting paid for services rendered was my idea of a real job. Real estate was a wonderful education. I even went on to earn my broker's license. Dad and I had four good years working together, but it was time to move on, so I put my license in escrow.

I decided to enroll in hair school after I saw an advertisement on television. I knew instantly that was what I wanted to try next. I figured I'd get paid for services rendered, as well as satisfy my artistic side. So I took out a student loan and began cosmetology school in September of '97.

My sister Angel had gone through a divorce after ten years of marriage, but she was doing amazing! She put herself through college and earned her teaching certificate as a single mom with two children. She was engaged to the manager of a local YMCA. Angel and her new man were into triathlons. She won the first one she ever entered and had competed in many by this time. She eventually qualified for and finished the Iron Man in Hawaii. Wow! A full Iron Man consists of a 2.4-mile swim and a 112-mile bike followed by a 26.2-mile marathon. She completed this distance in 12 hours and 15 minutes. Angel exposed me to fitness, and I was forever thankful to her.

Angel's fiancé hired me to work part-time in the fitness center of the YMCA, and this is where I worked while going to hair school. My job was to conduct orientations on the weight machines and cardio equipment. Soon, I became involved in Angel's water aerobics classes, started running a little, and fell in love with lifting weights. I didn't think smoking and drinking would allow me to enjoy these things, but I was wrong. That was what I called balance in my life now. Truly, getting the job at the YMCA was one of the best things that ever happened to me.

I'd been searching for some balance in the spiritual realm as well, the whole "meaning of life" thing. *What is this "something" we are all looking for? Why do I feel so empty?* Christianity and Jesus were the furthest thing from my mind. Throughout all my years of partying, God had zero relevance in my life. I was not sure there was a God. The way I thought of it, we were all alone; it was me, myself, and I and as long as I was doing what I wanted, life was as it should be.

My parents were no longer practicing Catholics, disenchanted with organized religion. They were searching—or should I say "lost"—like me? At this time, I was open to anything they were into. I had read some Deepak Chopra and Krishnamurti, books that my mom was into then. After having a discussion with my mom, I came to the conclusion that I am God, and God is I.

I recall Lauren becoming very upset and crying when I told her that I didn't believe in God, per se. She wanted to see me in Heaven because she loved me so. I didn't believe in Heaven, but maybe reincarnation. Who really knew about any of that stuff anyway? It was a mystery.

SPECIAL DELIVERY

I was almost thirty-two-years-old, living at my mom and dad's again, and starting hair school, which was absolute torture: nine to five, Monday through Friday for a full year with a bunch of immature young girls and a boy or two. I had to keep my eye on the prize, and getting stoned most days made it somewhat tolerable.

The majority of nights, I hit the bar with or without my girls, Lauren and Roxy. I loved visiting Junior and Scotty, my bartender friends. They knew me all too well, so if I happened to leave the bar without paying my tab, as I did once in a while, they never worried. I'd show up the next day and make good along with a big tip and apology. I couldn't help but get wrapped up in shooting pool, and I drank most nights for little to nothing so my tabs were never huge.

Lauren begged me to go out one night, but it had only been ten days since I'd moved out of Tom's. Believe it or not, I was not in the mood. I had a huge boil on my chin along with an array of other glorious pimples. We started at Junior and Scotty's bar, and I reluctantly followed her to our other watering hole, all the while stressing about the throbbing on my face. How could I forget about it? It was on the verge of eruption.

We got our beers and found a table. Lauren mentioned to me that a guy was staring at me. I didn't even look. I didn't care. I just wanted to wallow in my misery and suck down some beers. Five minutes later, Lauren told me he had not taken his eyes off of me except to take his shots at the pool table. Lauren insisted I just take a peek. When I turned around, sure enough, he was staring me down.

I supposed it wouldn't hurt to shoot a game of pool. I frequently ran the table there. He was standing, holding his pool cue. I walked up to him and asked, "How long before I can shoot?" He went up to the chalkboard and erased the six or seven names and said, "You're up next." *Pretty cool*, I thought; I hated having to wait.

He asked if he could buy me a beer, and I responded as I always did when I'm with my girls, "Only if you buy my friend a drink too." It worked like a charm as usual. Lauren, Roxy, and I were always on the lookout for drink fairies, and I seemed to be a magnet for them. I shot some pool and went back to my table, and he followed me. Darn it!

He recited poetry to me and, by the end of the night, had written me a lovely poem on a cocktail napkin. Didn't he even notice the boil that was consuming my face? I wished he would have left me alone.

He was very attractive in a Native American kind of way, with the nose of a great warrior chief and dark skin; he was fit, with a military haircut and an accent to die for. Not really my type, but I was intrigued. He bought Lauren and me the rest of our drinks that night. He asked for my phone number, and I actually gave it to him, which was not my usual style. He thought the number was bogus, questioning it several times, trying to catch me in a lie. If I didn't want someone to have it, I just said no. I ticked off my share of guys with that word.

He called me the next day, and we made a date. Juan picked me up at my parents with a half dozen red roses and another poem—the ultimate Latin lover.

Juan was born in Peru and moved to the United States after graduating from high school. His dad lived in Brooklyn, and Juan worked in New York City for a year before joining the Marine Corps. He learned to speak English under immense pressure in boot camp on Parris Island and then at Camp Lejeune, where he was stationed. He served in Desert Storm as frontline infantry. He went into the Marine Corps as a scrawny boy and came out a well-built and very proud man. He looked so fine in his fatigues and dress blues. After four years of active duty, he joined the reserves in Lansing, Michigan, and went to work for the postal service, eventually transferring to the Zoo. When I met him, he was a sergeant and had been in the reserves for six years. We had sex on our first date, and the romance was on.

I was impressed with what Juan had achieved. As a child in Peru, he worked in the fish market to help support his family, and had even made himself a pair of shoes before. I couldn't imagine. He wired money home every single month, still helping to provide for his mother and siblings. The night we met was the same night his brother Marlon came to live with him from

Peru. Marlon was eighteen and spoke no English. Juan had his hands full with the responsibility of preparing his little brother for life in the United States and taking on a new girlfriend.

The Marine Corps Ball was on my birthday that year, which was not long after we started dating. Of course, I called it my birthday ball. It was incredible and I gained even greater respect for all those who serve and had served our country.

Juan turned me on to country music. I'd been listening to heavy metal and classic rock for far too long. It was a nice change of pace, and for some reason, I picked up on the little bit of God that was in it. He even turned me on to Yanni and violin concertos. Not to worry, the boy could salsa too, *no problema*. He really opened up a whole new world to me.

An instructor at hair school warned me about jarheads, so she called them. She said to be careful, that they were all hotheads. I soon found out what she meant. Juan and I met at the bar to have some drinks a few weeks after we started dating. While there, I ran into an old girlfriend. I was out of weed, and she said we could get stoned at her house. Juan and I went our separate ways. I told him I'd meet him at his place after I did my thing.

Apparently, I took too long. When I was almost to Juan's house, he came out of nowhere and jumped on the hood of the car, screaming at me. I parked and got out, wondering what the hell was up with him. I had a pretty good buzz on and couldn't control my laughter. I didn't understand what the big deal was. I was just being me. He got really angry because I simply could not quit laughing at him. He dragged me into the house, threw me on the bed, and proceeded to choke me, all in front of his brother, who was screaming hysterically, in Spanish, of course. He finally backed off. I told him if he ever laid another hand on me, I would hire someone to break his legs, and he'd never see me again. Like a fool, I stayed the night. I tried real hard not to laugh at him anymore, but it wasn't always easy. Lauren said I should leave him.

Juan and I were together for three months when I missed a period—very odd—so I bought a pregnancy test. It was positive. I was thrilled and shocked. *What would Juan say?* I hadn't been on birth control for eight years. My only pregnancy almost killed me, and my chances of having a baby. So I thought. Juan was fully aware of this.

I showed him the test when he came home, and he was, shall I say, not happy. His dream was to be a world traveler, and a baby didn't fit those plans. He wanted me to have an abortion, and I flat out refused. I told him he had two options: marry me, or pay child support and I'd raise the baby on my own. He stepped up, and we were married when I was six months pregnant. I wore a black maternity dress I purchased for four dollars at a consignment shop, and we were married at the local courthouse, with my mom and my dad as our witnesses.

I found out I was pregnant just two weeks before I had to go to the state board and test for my cosmetology license. I passed but decided not to work at a salon while

I was pregnant because of the chemicals, so I continued to work at the YMCA instead.

Our daughter, Aubrey, was born, July 27, 1999, four weeks after we were married and six weeks premature. The ob-gyn was right—my cervix couldn't handle the pressure. That's what I got for being promiscuous. STDs are a guarantee if you are sleeping around. I liked to think that Aubrey just couldn't wait to meet me!

The pregnancy was quite stressful—first, because Juan was still not crazy about the idea, and second, because we had to figure out how his brother Marlon was going to fit into the mix. It was far from the ideal situation I'd always dreamed of—being married first and then actually planning to get pregnant.

I pushed my daughter out in twenty-five minutes and broke every blood vessel from my chest up and did it without any drugs at all. I had to get her out fast, concerned that the delivery would be too hard on her. She weighed four pounds, fourteen ounces. I dreamt I was having a girl, so I knew before we ever had the ultrasound. Aubrey looked just like in my dream, only smaller. She was so beautiful, with tons of dark hair.

Two days after Aubrey was born, Juan left for California for two weeks. He couldn't get out of the Marine Corps Super Squad Competition. His troop had worked hard to earn their spot there, and he was the squad leader.

I spent all the time they allowed me at the hospital. I fed my daughter through a tube in her nose and went through the motions of breast-feeding her several times a day because her brain was not developed enough to have that natural instinct. I gave Aubrey her first bath with the help of a nurse. I crocheted a baby blanket for her in the hospital and stared at her in her Isolette, so in love with her yet almost afraid to touch her. She looked so fragile.

She latched onto my breast at exactly two weeks, and Dad helped me bring her home. I had to buy a special insert, so she would fit in the car seat. Dad called her the potato queen because, of course, Dad would tell you that potatoes are indigenous to Peru, and there are over 1,100 varieties—a little bit of trivia he picked up somewhere. I preferred to think of her as my Incan princess.

She was on an apnea monitor for the first three weeks she was home. She had to have wires attached to her 24-7, and when the monitor went off, as it did a couple of times, I had to nudge her so she would start breathing again. I was terrified when she no longer needed the device, and I watched her like a hawk for days.

I had one or two drinks from time to time during my pregnancy. My doctor said that was fine, and I happened to quit smoking six weeks before I found out I was pregnant, one of dozens of attempts over the twenty-plus years that I'd been smoking. I had no desire to smoke during my pregnancy and only did a tiny bit while breast feeding. My motherly instincts kicked right in, and I found that miraculous.

While breast-feeding, I rented a pump and stockpiled milk in the freezer. Now I could get drunk without doing any harm to Aubrey, and it gave Juan an opportunity to feed her too. I started smoking full-time again after she finished breast-feeding at about five months. Could it be she didn't like the taste of my milk anymore as I gradually started smoking again?

Juan was scheduled to leave the country with his Marine Corps unit for several weeks just after Y2K when Aubrey was five-months-old. I didn't want him in the Marine Corps anymore. I hadn't really forgiven him for not being there the first two weeks, and the thought of Aubrey losing her dad was unbearable. Juan was not afraid to put his life on the line for the great US of A. He reluctantly quit. Aubrey was very important to Juan after he finally met her, but I wasn't sure he'd ever forgive me for pushing him to quit the Corps.

When I was pregnant, we discussed having two or three children, but his tune changed after I had Aubrey. I never wanted an only child. Kids needed siblings like I had. Well, maybe not exactly like I had. I told Juan that if Aubrey was going to be an only child, he was going to have to work his fanny off because I was going to be a stay-at-home mom. I wasn't going to miss out on anything if this was my only opportunity to be a mother. I quit the YMCA and stayed home for the first three years of Aubrey's life. It was the best decision I had ever made. I loved taking care of my baby girl full-time, as hard as it was. She grew very quickly. Aubrey started out in the fifth percentile for weight and by six months of age she was in the ninetieth percentile. You would have never guessed she was a preemie anymore.

We sold Juan's home and purchased a home in a brand-new development. The basement was just being poured when we bought it, and I was able to bird-dog the whole process and make a few upgrades such as laminated wood flooring, a skylight, and white trim. Most new homes had oak trim, and in my opinion, oak made a house show like a trailer. I had a natural ability for decorating, and I was into Feng Shui at the time; it was kind of my new religion. As long as everything was in balance, things would come together.

When Aubrey was eighteen-months-old, I was pushing to have another child again. I was thirty-five and definitely not getting any younger. Juan's response was to have a vasectomy. I signed the consent papers and let him do his thing, crushed beyond repair. That was the beginning of the end for us.

WINTER IN PERU

We took Aubrey to Peru for her second birthday. Juan insisted on taking several thousand dollars of spending money. I didn't understand until we got there. No amount of explaining could have prepared me for what I was about to experience. We arrived at Juan's family home in Calloa outside of Lima via a taxi. It was a free-for-all on the roads; a matter of who was the biggest bully. Traffic lights were simply ignored. I couldn't believe my eyes and held on to Aubrey as tightly as I could without hurting her. I needed a drink.

Juan's home was brick, cement, and dirt. The town was filthy. There was no grass or trees to speak of. The windows had bars, and the yard was a cement slab. Portions of the house had no roof. In the kitchen, the ceiling was made of fiberglass sheets that leaked.

We went in our summer, their winter, and it was the season of *garua*, a light mist of rain that seemed never ending. The cement floors were damp and slippery. We slept upstairs, and the two-story cement staircase was completely open, meaning no railings. Of course, it was Aubrey's favorite place to play. Not the ideal environment for an active two-year-old. I was on pins and needles the entire two weeks.

I was wary of most of the food but fell in love with the avocados while there. They were so yummy with the fresh *pan* (bread) we purchased every day, and luckily for me, there was a *tienda* (convenience store) on every other corner in this neighborhood. I bought liters of beer for a buck to calm my nerves. I was rarely without a bottle of Cristal or Cusqueña in my hand. Hey, I'd have double-fisted it if I thought I could get away with it. It was hard to describe how depressed I felt when down there. I hated the strong hold alcohol had on me, but I didn't know what else to do.

Juan's dad, Papa Beto, who lived in New York City at the time sent money down to Peru so, for the very first time, they would have a refrigerator and washing machine before we arrived—for *our* comfort, not theirs. How beautiful was that? I fell in love with these people.

Oh, Juan's family was poor, but not the poorest of poor by Peru's standards. They did not know any different and were content with the little they had, working sunup to sundown just to feed themselves that day. I understood why Juan brought all the money. I spent hours shopping in the markets with *my* list of their needs, which were many, such as a mirror for the bathroom and a shelf for their toiletries. The bathroom was a big tile stall with a floor drain, sink, and toilet. To bathe, you had to heat up a large pot of water on the stove and take it to the stall. You get the picture.

Only one person in Juan's entire family owned a vehicle. They were a luxury. One of Juan's sisters and I took a cab to the shopping district in downtown Lima, and I hooked her up with some clothing and shoes for her and the family. The downtown was beautiful, but one block outside of downtown, I saw a child pooping in the street. What a difference a block made.

I was not able to communicate much with Juan's family. They spoke no English, and the Spanish classes I took prior to the trip were basically useless because they talked so freaking fast. I could say "Mas cerveza, por favor!" (More beer, please!), "Rapido!" (Fast.), "Que rico!" (Yummy!), and "Donde esta el baño?" (Where is the bathroom?). These important phrases came in handy.

I came back with a much greater appreciation of my country as well as feelings of guilt. It never truly sank in how blessed we were in the USA until that trip. My annoying problems with substance abuse seemed trivial in comparison to so many things. I easily justified my condition, because things *could* be so much worse, like being impoverished, undernourished *and* a drunk.

THE MUGGING

Many events left me pondering the existence of God; Angel, Timothy, Peter, and Joy, to name a few, but none hit closer to home then the random act of thievery, that very nearly took my mother's life. And a bizarre connection that always puzzled me.

My mother was the victim of a purse snatching. She worked in downtown Kalamazoo; she routinely had her hair done at a nearby salon. That night, two salon employees were escorting my mom to her car in a lot a couple of blocks away. It was evening and winter time so it was beginning to get dark when the three of them were making their way through the narrow alley into the lot. This large lot doubled as a concert site in the summer months.

While walking between her escorts, two people ran up from behind and snatched Mom's purse, violently flinging her backward onto the pavement head first. The assailants got away while Mom lay on the pavement with a major head injury.

I received a call and rushed to the emergency room. The hospital happened to be right downtown, in the vicinity of the mugging. When I arrived I was led to a room. My mom lay on a table, incoherent and moaning and groaning, her head twice the normal size. She reminded me of the Elephant Man. This image was forever etched in my brain. Dad and the surgeon were looking at x-rays and discussing Mom's fragile state.

I showed up just in time to hear the surgeon say, "If we don't do surgery within the next half an hour she will die."

I spoke calmly. "Do it." Dad was a bit reluctant and told the surgeon that Mom would not want any scars to show. The surgeon very compassionately reassured both of us that all the scarring would be behind the hairline but they would have to shave her head. Then the surgeon explained that the incision would start at the forehead on the right side and end behind her right ear. Mom was whisked away.

When Dad and I returned to the waiting room, I remember Angel being there. She was a total wreck, unable to control the sobbing, and she asked me how I was keeping it all together. I responded with a big hug and told her that Mom was going to be okay. I was a wreck too, but couldn't let it show. I tried not to allow negative thoughts to take over. I had to keep it together for Dad. I was concerned about him as well.

For the next several week's I was *Dad's* rock. I didn't allow him to spend too much time alone. I brought movies over to watch with him. I hung out as much as my schedule allowed. We visited mom in rehab and those were always the hardest days. He told me a number of times that he didn't know if he could go on without her. When he wept I held his hand.

Initially, Mom didn't know who we were. The physical therapy was long and intense. It was painful, but I never doubted she would recover. As far as anyone could tell, she had made a full recovery. If I asked Mom, she may not agree.

Silent Observer offered the largest reward ever at that time, for any information leading to arrest of the perpetrators, and they were apprehended within days of the incident.

My mom insisted on saying a few words in court prior to their sentencing. Mom asked that the court go easy on these young men because they did not intend to harm her, only to snatch her purse. Dad sat and listened, still dealing with his anger. I couldn't understand how Mom could be so forgiving. The portion of her brain that shows compassion was obviously still intact.

This was the bizarre part which would only mean anything to me. Verve Pipe, a local band that I followed from their beginning, turned big time and performed that summer in this very lot where the mugging occurred. The name of the new album they were promoting was of all things, "I've Suffered a Head Injury." What a trip! I went to the concert and spent most of the time holding back tears, knowing that I could have just as easily been standing on my mother's chalk line.

I felt the depth of Mom's scar; a long, narrow, crevice in her skull, left behind from the brain surgery. I was filled with a deep sense of gratitude every time my fingers or comb came in contact with the remnants of the mugging. She pulled through, and I was all the better for it! Maybe I had God to thank for that?

CHANGE IS GOOD?

Being a mother, I attempted to quit drinking, but failed miserably, time and time again. I was able to moderate my drinking for a time, and would only have a six-pack of beer or a couple of forty ounce bottles a day. This was pretty tame by my standards.

A lovely Christian neighbor invited me to a women's Christmas candlelight dessert at her church. I was curious, so I went. I'm sure she could tell I needed saving. I do not recall much of what took place during the event; I was preoccupied. Regrettably, I drank several beers before she picked me up that evening, and I couldn't wait to get home so I could have some more. What a shame.

But, I really did have this longing to raise Aubrey in a church, not that I needed it. I just wanted to give her the same opportunity I had, and she could make her own decision when she got older.

Juan wanted nothing to do with church. He was raised Catholic too, but had a horrible experience in New York with a so-called Christian. As a result, Juan came to the conclusion that the church was full of hypocrites, and of course, he was right. Our neighbor invited us to attend their church on a couple of occasions and I graciously declined. Juan wouldn't go, and I didn't push the issue. As a result, I gave up on the idea.

—⚜—

Three years into our marriage, Juan and I were in constant conflict. When I said black, he said white. Our relationship was a disaster and I was miserable. Juan's negative perspective on life and people was sucking me down. He was a bitter man with a huge chip on his shoulder, and I was over being interrogated and controlled.

I started to have more frequent girls' nights out. Juan also had his nights out. He began accusing me of fooling around on him, which was the last thing I'd ever do unless fooling around with drugs and alcohol counted. I had never fooled around on anybody. I had waited until my divorce was final with Timothy, and I would do the same with Juan.

I began making my escape plan. Aubrey was three-years-old and starting preschool, so I started working at a salon and went back to work at the YMCA. It took a long time to complete the plan. When Aubrey started kindergarten, it was time to make my move.

Juan and I had very infrequent sex for the last two years of our marriage. I only did it out of obligation, which was a tragic place to be. That October, I told him I was divorcing him and would stay until the end of the year for Aubrey's sake. I wanted the holidays to be as normal as possible for her. We still slept in the same bed, with little chance of Juan getting laid anymore.

This was one of the greatest disappointments in my life. Why couldn't he have been the man I could spend the rest of my life with? Maybe there was no such person. Sad to say, most of my family was not supportive of my move. I didn't care though. It was my life, and I had made up my mind. The fighting was frequent, and I had two pet names for Juan and they were very inappropriate—not words I wanted my child to grow up remembering.

I could only hope that my daughter would someday know what a loving relationship was really like. Juan warned me that if I ever tried to take Aubrey away from him, he would kill me, and I believed him. I wanted Aubrey to have a relationship with her dad. I would agree to joint custody.

SINGLE MESS

Aubrey and I moved into Mom and Dad's temporarily until the divorce was final. Talk about a revolving door. My parents were in Las Vegas for six months, so it worked out beautifully. I had my real estate broker's license, and as sole proprietor, I was able to do my own deals so I would buy a house as soon as the divorce was settled.

When *The Apprentice* came out, Roxy said I could win it with my street smarts, real estate background, and great personality. Whatever! If she only knew what a piece of poop I really felt like. And sorry, Donald, but I'd have been fired for advising you about your hair. Yikes! *Survivor* was another show Roxy thought I'd be sure to win, but heaven forbid I give up smoking and drinking for fifteen minutes of fame.

I got an amazing deal on a fixer-upper from an acquaintance who owned several income properties, and I made a good bit of money on it in a little over a year. Common sense went a long way when dealing in real estate, and my flair for interior design didn't hurt, and I had an eye for detail; it was *all* about the details.

I could do this on my own—that is, be a single mom. I didn't need much, and money was never a huge motivator for me. My happiness and having fun, as in partying hard, was always the ultimate goal. I always partied like it was 1999, no matter what the year.

Lauren and I were out drinking again; this time at a piano bar in downtown Kalamazoo. Lauren pointed out a very attractive man at the end of the bar looking at me. Why did she do that? I preferred not to notice those things. As we were leaving, Lauren, who was very married, told this hottie our plans to hit another bar around the corner, which was basically an invitation for him to follow, and he did, to my horror. I wasn't at all interested in getting to know him *until* he said he worked for the United States Tennis Association (USTA) and was in the Zoo for the Boys Nationals. My ex-fiancé Tom introduced me to tennis. I started playing when I was thirty-six years old and was immediately hooked, and was currently playing a minimum of four hours a week.

The USTA Boys Nationals tennis tournament is the oldest and most prestigious of all of the junior boys' tennis championships. Most of the greats have played in this tournament: McEnroe, Connors, Chang, Agassi, Roddick, and Querrey just to name a few.

I was once again intrigued by good looks and an accent to die for. He lived in LA but was South African. We talked tennis until the bar closed, and he invited me to his hotel room. The following evening, he came over to my place, and we drank, got stoned, and what have you, and I gave him my first ever topless haircut. He loved drugs and alcohol and wanted me to try and score some cocaine, to no avail. We shared drug war stories. I was completely unaware that Viagra was a popular drug in the bar scene in LA. That was news to me, but wasn't it human nature to find a way to abuse things, especially sexual enhancement drugs? Whoever invented that drug had high hopes for it being abused, no doubt, and the bottom line was greed. Some of the biggest drug pushers advertise right in our media. He might have been on some Viagra that weekend, come to think of it. He was a little too excitable.

On top of doing hair as a single mom, I was an experienced painter now, and really enjoyed it. I painted for friends and family on the side to help supplement my income. I was paying my bills. What more could I have asked for?

Well, I wanted a boob job, something Juan would not allow when we were married. I swore to myself I'd never have sex on top again until I had them done. Being on the bottom was not that appealing either. I had two empty sacks now between the breast-feeding and fairly low percentage of body fat, due to lifting weights and playing tons of tennis. I was on court up to eight hours a week.

I was thirty-eight when I got my "refills" and paid cash for them. I went smaller than the surgeon recommended. He told me I'd want them bigger after I got them and that every woman did. He was wrong. I did not want to look like a porn star—thank you very much—and I'd look ridiculous on the tennis court, not to mention they might get in the way. I opted for a C cup as I had been accustomed to in my youth. I also had my belly button pierced to help hide the scar from the laparoscopy associated with my ectopic pregnancy.

I was trying to make the best of my life, keeping a positive attitude, something I always strived to do. My most common nickname now, was Smiley. I'd actually been criticized many times for being too happy. There was something wrong with that statement. I'd also been told numerous times that I had a very positive energy. People told me they started feeling better when they hung around me. That was a wonderful compliment. I'd been described as being very real. Yeah, real high! I'd even been told a few times that I had a beautiful aura. I guess I was just born that way, like other people seem to be born into depression.

My dear sister Angel was going through some major struggles with depression at this time that I was fully unaware of until this night. It was Danny's fortieth birthday party at a very fine-dining establishment in downtown Grand Rapids where his wife Rachel worked. I was having a lovely time, drinking my beers and visiting. When I went to the restroom to freshen up, I ran into Angel. She was crying, so I approached her and put my hand on her shoulder. I mentioned the fact that it was sad to me that she was often crying lately; then, I inquired about her depression medication. If looks could kill, I'd have been dead on the floor. She unleashed her demons on me again. She shoved me as hard as she could into the wall and proceeded to kick my butt as she screamed at me, cursing me up and down, telling me how much she hated me. She hated me for *caring*? I defended myself as best I could, with no attempt to fight back. She was using me as a punching bag.

The poor manager heard the commotion and came in and pulled her off of me. Angel ran out the door. My fear was that she would find the highest building and jump off. I was not sure what just happened and what she might be capable of. She was nowhere to be seen, so I sent Danny to find her, and I was out of there. The party was *over*. My head and my face were bumped and bruised, and my hair was a mess. Darn it, and I was having a good hair day. Really, I was absolutely devastated.

SIMPLY OUTRAGEOUS

I was still working at the salon; I'd been there for three and a half years. Our sweet manager was fired when we were bought out by the largest salon chain in the USA. We had a new manager, and I was concerned for my job. The new boss was a miserable older man I'd worked with the entire time, and he wanted me out of there. He'd been doing hair for over twenty-five years and hated everybody and his job. I felt for the guy and tried to be a friend. Apparently, his first course of action as manager was to get rid of me. I had wonderful client retention and was one of the most successful stylists, but that didn't stop him. When I showed up for work that fated day, the regional manager was there. I was called into the break room, and the ax fell. My new boss said he had received a complaint from a client that I was being *too sexual*. Ha. I told him in front of the regional manager that he knew it was total BS, while he turned twelve shades of red. I'd never been fired before. As a matter of fact, I'd always been a star employee. The regional manager told me to grab my things and leave immediately.

    I received a phone call that evening from the top stylist, who was shocked and saddened. She left with another stylist a month later and joined a salon around the corner.

Luckily, I had a lot of painting jobs lined up, and I avoided the salon business for several months. I would have to start over almost entirely because I had no way of contacting my clients. My girl at the salon, bless her heart, did the best she could the last month she was there to pass along my phone number illegally to anyone who inquired about me. I had a used hair chair and maintained a dozen or so clients in my dining room for the time being. That was a far cry from the two hundred–plus clients I use to have.

—∞—

The guy who sold me my house wound up being a cocaine and meth connection. It wouldn't hurt to do some once in a while. I made it through fourteen years touching barely any powder. Refusing a line at this point was what I would have considered drug abuse, much like spilling a beer would be alcohol abuse. When I didn't have Aubrey, I overindulged. I picked up a gram of cocaine whenever I could afford it, and I drank heavily, pushing a case of beer a day. I'd hardly missed a day of drinking since Aubrey was born, same as before my pregnancy. It was just the norm for me. I still enjoyed the one-y I purchased at the Hash Bash at age twenty-two, and it was a part of me, like a beer in hand.

I was forty-years-old and happily single, I suppose. I definitely never planned on marrying again. I was set in my ways. I had a premonition that I shared with many people over the years about dying prematurely. I figured

I'd be lucky to make it to fifty. I resigned myself to living in this manner for the rest of my life and wouldn't want to involve anyone else. *I am what I am.* My destiny had already been determined, and I was okay with that. I'd lived a full life—been there, done that.

I hoped that Aubrey would help me clean up my act, but I was only getting worse. I was a really good mom despite my affliction, working twice as hard to be a good parent. My child was not going to be a spoiled, rotten brat, if I had anything to do with it. When I said no, I meant it. She never had a temper tantrum and was a sweet, compassionate little girl. She was my angel, and fortunately, she never witnessed her mother falling down drunk or belligerent. That was just not my style. I was all about control, and it was becoming a serious challenge.

I actually smoked a little crack for the first time as a single mom and was not impressed. I was obviously a snob. Freebasing was better. I was also doing some of the dirty meth that didn't even slightly resemble the stuff of yesteryear. Frankly, it was frightening. I smoked some too on several different occasions. That didn't impress me either. I suppose I was just feeling my age. It sure was plentiful and easy to find. I knew several modern-day meth addicts. They were easy to spot. No such thing as a slow fade when you are messing around with that garbage. I'd watched it destroy some lives fast. I wasn't looking to go *that* route.

I was taking my time killing myself with alcohol, talk about a slow fade. One day, I had a brilliant idea about my drinking. Instead of beer, because it was really getting out of hand, I would change to whiskey, and why not Jack Daniel's? I backed off the hard liquor quite some time ago. Shots were off limits most of the time because I might lose my good sense, and real alcoholics drank the hard stuff. I chose beer as the healthier, safer option, but it hadn't been working for me lately. I wound up going through a gallon of Jack Daniel's in the first week, but then decided it was best to go back to my beer. Plus, I heard from an old alcoholic acquaintance that the brown liquor was hardest on the liver. I thanked him for the tip. It was definitely a different buzz, and I enjoyed it for about a minute.

It was frightening to think that I had been drunk driving for twenty-five years now. I'd been doing it since age fifteen. In recent summers, I never left home without a small cooler stocked with beer; and in the winters, I'd throw them in a bag. It didn't matter if it was seven a.m. I had cold ones waiting for me when I got off the tennis court for a liquid lunch. Sucking down a six-pack in an hour or so was just normal for me. I tied one on quickly and maintained my buzz for the rest of the day and night. There was no break time, and this ritual included staying stoned as well. I guarded my tennis for the time being, not wanting to ruin my focus with a buzz. I didn't suffer from hangovers when I stuck to beer. I rarely got headaches, and I was lucky to have been born with a rock gut. I had this drinking thing down to a science. I considered myself a freak of nature. I *did* start having loose bowels and an occasional dry heave in the morning, but nothing I couldn't handle.

I would have to say, my lowest point as a single mom was when a couple empty beer cans fell out in the parking lot at Aubrey's school. I was picking her up from school, and I was directly outside the main door. School just let out and all the parents, students, and teachers were outside. Aubrey opened the passenger door to get in. I didn't realize I had chucked so many empty beer cans under the passenger seat, and there they fell for all the world to see. I couldn't get out and run around the car and pick up those cans quick enough! I made sure not to look up and make eye contact with anybody. Aubrey thought nothing of it. She was used to seeing mommy's beer cans—so much shame. How did I ever believe that was acceptable? I had been drinking and driving with Aubrey since she was an infant. I had it under control. I was the best one-eyed drunk driver too, but only when necessary. Practice makes perfect. I watched the speed limit closely and had a hawk eye for cops. I could spot a cop from a mile away.

I was working back at the YMCA part-time and earned my personal training certificate. For the last couple years, I was using health and wellness products that my mom and dad turned me on to. The protein shakes and cleanses were phenomenal. This stuff was keeping me healthy. I was eating well, focusing on protein shakes, Omega 3s, spinach, homemade trail mix, and yogurt. I rarely ate French fries, potato chips or fast-food. That junk will kill you. Have I mention that I'm a hypocrite? This was again, my twisted balance. Eat right, exercise, drink, drug, and smoke.

My boss at the YMCA could not believe how fit I was. He considered me to be an athlete, and he knew all my dirty secrets. He was a long-time friend and almost my brother-in-law, and he gave me a warning about drinking on the job. He was more concerned about someone smelling me, not that I couldn't do my job. He supplied me with gum to make himself feel better, and I behaved as best I could. I worked for him for eleven years, and the YMCA was my home away from home. I loved my job and was an excellent employee, running circles around everyone else. The Y helped me to feel normal, and it seemed a good cover-up for my outrageous lifestyle.

KEN DOLL

Lauren's husband, Don, was a commercial electrician, and he was anxious for me to meet one of his foremen. Don told me his only criticism of this guy, Kenny, was that he was *too* nice. Kenny had recently been through a rough divorce after nineteen years of marriage, and Don had witnessed the turmoil Kenny was going through, sometimes breaking down at work and unable to hide his pain.

Lauren and Don had a housewarming party and said I could meet him there. Problem was, he was already in a rebound relationship, and all I ever saw of him that night was the back of his head while he was making out with his new gal pal on the family room sofa.

Many months later, I was doing some painting at Don and Lauren's. It was a good-size job: living room, dining room, kitchen, and family room. Don used to bird-dog me and, apparently, shared with Kenny what a marvelous painter I was. Kenny was available again and decided to use painting as a ploy to meet me. He called to ask me if I could come to his home and give an estimate. Aubrey and I drove to Lawton, about half an hour away, on a Sunday afternoon. I drank several beers before arriving and brought my cooler with me. I had no idea what to expect and drove past his home. It stood out like a sore thumb.

When I finally figured it out, I pulled in the driveway and Kenny walked out of the garage. He appeared arrogant, living in a gorgeous home in the midst of a bunch of fixer-uppers. We went inside so he could show me the dining room and bathroom he wanted painted. We looked at paint swatches and the new ceramic tile for the floor he was going to lay in the bathroom. He certainly needed help decorating. The dining room wallpaper was covered with a gazillion little red flowers that made me dizzy, and the bathroom had plaid wallpaper and vine stenciling.

We decided on the color over a couple of beers, which I considered a big bonus. He gave me the code to the front door that day. He offered to take me out to dinner for having to drive so far, but I blew him off. There had to be something wrong with this guy! I *did* discover however during our first meeting that he was shy and nervous and far from arrogant. You can't always trust your first impression.

—⁂—

I was finally working at a new salon. I needed the income. I ran into Danny's old girlfriend Lisa, the one that got me the job at Dunkin' Donuts so many years ago. Her nail tech's friend had just opened a salon and was looking for her first hairdresser. It was time to get back into the hair business. These two nail techs were a hoot. They both liked to drink and offered wine to their clients. Some of their clients even brought in their own booze, with blenders and all. I could bring my beers and keep them in the fridge and offer my clients a drink if I wanted. Business was decent, and I was free to drink at work. They loved my hair skills and I loved the fact that they specialized in Tammy Taylor pink and white sculpted nails and on occasion we traded services.

I'd been working at the salon for about a year when I finally shared with these nail techs that I had a drinking problem. They just couldn't see it. Nobody could. They were lushes and got sloppy. Not this pro. I told them I needed to go to rehab or something. I was getting very burned out and desperately wanted it to end. Lisa was there getting her nails done and was very cold with this self-righteous, get-over-it attitude. She obviously didn't hear what I was saying. She was also sloppy. It hurt my feelings, and I became visibly upset during a discussion. She asked why I couldn't just stop at three or four. That's what I wanted to know! I made frequent attempts to quit over the years, and all quickly failed.

Addiction was a very tough concept to understand for individuals who had not experienced it themselves. I couldn't stop, no matter how hard I tried. I didn't have the willpower. I was weak. I should have been able to do this on my own. I was God, right? I should be able to fix me. Why weren't all the Deepak Chopra and Krishnamurti teachings helping me? Meditate, be one with the universe, blah, blah, blah. I was just spiritually *inept*, I guess. My life was out of control, and I hated it.

―∞―

I was in a new home now, my next flipper. Things were going great in regard to Aubrey and my financial life, and I continued to count the blessings I did have. When

I was feeling down, I could put things in perspective. Things could always be worse. I had to keep the glass half full. I *was* an upper.

It was slow at the salon one Friday evening, so I called Kenny to take him up on his offer to have dinner. It had been a few weeks since we'd met at his place, and he had asked me out several more times. I guess it was time to give the guy a break. When I called, he was having drinks with the boys. I could tell he was very excited, with the boys jeering in the background.

He picked me up at my home that evening in his white (chariot) Chevy Silverado, and we went to one of my favorite dive bars. They had awesome blues bands and two pool tables I was familiar with. Kenny and I started shooting pool, and he quickly discovered I was good. I easily won the first couple of games, and he started poking me with his stick. I was getting angry and *very* seriously told him if he poked me one more time, we were through. Period! He heeded my warning. We were intoxicated, and I invited him to spend the night so he didn't have to drive drunk all the way home. I told him he could sleep on the futon in the living room, but my bed would be more comfortable. We weren't planning on having sex that night, but we did, as awkward as it was. At least we got that over with. What a horrible attitude.

Within three weeks, we were sure this relationship was right. We'd both been divorced over two years, with no intentions of ever getting married again. I was very upfront with Kenny about where I was at. I gave him all the gory details about my past and present party habits and the fact that I could very well drink and smoke myself to death. I told him that I had no idea what the future held for me, and he must promise to love me *no matter what.* Don warned Kenny that I was a "wild child," as he put it, but I don't think Kenny was expecting all that.

I made previous arrangements to spend the weekend at Lake Michigan with a group of my party buds and invited Kenny to come with me. I warned him I would be indulging in cocaine, and he watched me do lines all weekend long. Kenny was a small-town boy. We grew up on opposite sides of the tracks. The most he'd ever done was drink beer and smoke a little pot when he was a kid, and he drank in moderation as an adult. He had a lot of the same qualities that I loved in my first husband, Timothy. He was brilliant, shy, and innocent with a naive quality that I respected.

Kenny just so happened to be smokin' hot and very well put together for a forty-something man, as well. I was usually attracted to younger men because most of the guys I knew who were my age had beer guts. Kenny was three years older than me, and you could actually see his abdominal muscles. He was a Christian, and when he told me he went to church, I was very excited. I couldn't wait to check it out. Kenny had something I wanted. He was such a peaceful, loving man, and well grounded. If only I could tap into it.

Kenny was also a very brave man. He was going on a work-related trip to Las Vegas two weeks after we started dating. My parents were living there full-time now and I encouraged Kenny to contact them while he was there. He would soon see Vegas like he never had before.

Mom and Dad picked him up at his casino on the Strip and took him for a champagne breakfast at the new Red Rock Casino, then to Red Rock Canyon and on a tour of their gorgeous retirement community. They also played a little blackjack, Kenny's favorite game coincidentally. He spent the whole day with a couple of old folks he didn't know from Adam. Now that took guts. My parents immediately picked up on his fine qualities. Dad's advice to me: "Don't screw this one up!" Funny thing was, I couldn't help but think that I probably would. What was Kenny doing with the likes of me?

THIRD TIME'S A CHARM

This was a pivotal time in my life and attending church with Kenny was exactly what I needed to get me going in the right direction. When we attended church, I chose where we sat. Kenny normally sat on the main floor, somewhere in the middle. I was barely comfortable in the balcony. At least the roof didn't cave in when I walked through the door. I sure felt like it should. I liked the pastor right away and listened intently to the sermons each Sunday. It was as if he was speaking directly to me. I cried during every service but was okay with that. I just didn't want anyone to see me.

We attended a marriage seminar based on Dr. Emerson Eggerichs's *Love and Respect* book and DVD. We had not tied the knot yet, but we went to all the sessions and found the material very enlightening. For Christmas that year, I sent all my siblings the book, not knowing where any of them were in relation to God but figuring it couldn't hurt. They were all married.

Kenny and I married on October 27, 2006, exactly six months after our first date. We were married at a courthouse with Don and Lauren as our witnesses, and our four children attended. We invited close friends and family to a bar afterward, where we partied the rest of the night away. We planned on having a big reception later that summer at our home. I sold my home in the Zoo and moved to Lawton where Kenny was born and raised.

Kenny's parents were salt of the earth, so the Atwater name was well respected in this small community. They passed away in the mid-nineties. I regretted not having a chance to meet them, but had on many occasions visited them in the cemetery, down the road a piece, and thanked them with teary eyes for raising such a fine boy.

Lily, Kenny's oldest child, was twenty-years-old when we met and lived in the apartment over the garage with a girlfriend. She loved to party, had plans to go to hair school, and was working at Big T's ever since high school.

Matt, Kenny's middle child, was eighteen and a prodigal, living with his mom a few blocks away. He was a high school dropout and not doing anything with his life at the time. I was much different than this dropout. He liked to party too, and I could definitely understand that.

Sad to say, in the beginning, I got stoned and drunk with Lily and Matt from time to time without Kenny's knowledge. I was worse than his kids. Somehow I always felt I earned the right to party with whomever I liked. I obviously was not a positive role model. My actions were a blatant indication of how lost I was.

Kenny's youngest child, Clare, was fourteen. She had the difficult task of moving in and out every two weeks. Luckily, her mom was close by. A sweet young girl, it was obvious Clare had made the decision early on to choose a narrower path than her older siblings. She was involved in her church youth groups, which included going on work camps.

The kids took me in stride. I would never know what it felt like to have a wicked stepmother. Aubrey was okay with Kenny, but I could see she had concerns about her dad's feelings and was not going to get too close to her stepfather. It was tough for Kenny and me, but we both realized we would never replace our stepchildren's parents. No matter how much we loved them, we couldn't let our expectation blur their reality. Kenny and I were not products of divorce.

Aubrey had her own room upstairs and she loved the idea of having brothers and sisters. She was seven when Kenny and I married. Aubrey and I had a beautiful home now, more than I could have ever imagined for us, with a large green lawn, a wraparound deck, and a swimming pool to boot.

Lawton was a small community with a population of about two thousand, surrounded by vineyards and a not-so-booming Welch's plant. It felt like a bit of Tuscany, I imagined, with the smell of grapes during harvest. It was breathtaking. Lawton was probably best known for a popular restaurant/bar, Big T's. They offered two hundred and fifty-five flavors of bottled beer, and you could join the beer club, and after you drank at least 130 varieties, you had VIP status. The membership was around 2,500 people. They sold a T-shirt that said, "If beer was a religion, this would be holy ground." Yep.

In the summer, Main Street was lined with Harleys, and you could feel the rumbling from our home. In the winter, snowmobiles took the place of the motorcycles.

Kenny's home was his project for the last twenty-plus years. He was a licensed commercial electrician, but was also a jack-of-all-trades. He had completely remodeled the house and the barn. The barn served as a garage with an apartment up above.

Kenny was in the process of finishing the siding on the barn when we started dating, and I offered my assistance. Hey, I was good at it, and Kenny empowered me. As far as he was concerned, there was nothing I couldn't do. He told me I was the best apprentice he ever had, and he meant it. He really believed in me, and being blessed with a bit of common sense didn't hurt either. I liked to tease Kenny that his garage was the biggest tool shed in Lawton. He had every tool you could imagine, and he was not afraid to use them. Handymen were such a turn-on!

Kenny allowed me to put my touch on the house. The rest of the plaid wallpaper and lovely stenciling would soon disappear along with some of the furnishings. It was feeling more like my home now, with the exception of all the oak trim, doors, and cabinets, which went against my grain. The oak was there to stay, so I had to get over it. At least the house did not show like a trailer. Kenny did beautiful work.

I was feeling quite spoiled and undeserving, and was still trying to figure out what Kenny saw in me. Yeah, I had some good qualities, I suppose, but I couldn't stop the drinking and drugging. I spent a lot of time beating myself up about it. I didn't have any excuse to numb myself anymore. I still loved the new buzz of the day but hated spending the rest of the day and night chasing that initial feeling that I could *never* get back. I had it all and wanted desperately to quit doing what I was doing. I owed it to Kenny and Aubrey to be the wife and mother they deserved, not that I was at all mean or abusive—but I had some huge issues. Quitting wasn't that easy.

I was still working at the salon and was unhappy in that environment, but moving to a different salon was out of the question. I would lose clients, and that was the last thing I wanted. Kenny gave me a gift to keep at the salon. It was a tiny pewter easel that had, "I Can Do All Things" (Philippians 4:13) on it, with a stack of cards in it that I could rotate, each with a different scripture. It was all Greek to me, but the thought was beautiful.

Kenny was planting seeds everywhere I turned; next was a mug. On one side, it read, "For I know the plans I have for you, says the Lord. Plans for good and not for evil, to give you a future and a hope" (Jeremiah 29:11). The word *journey* was on the opposite side. He seemed to know something I didn't. God had a plan for my wretched soul? That was hard to believe. I'd often thought I would make a good substance abuse counselor. I could definitely tell kids what *not* to do, but getting clean and sober would be a daunting task, if at all achievable.

—⚒—

Kenny came home one day and told me he found a salon for me in Lawton. You're kidding, right? The population was two thousand, with two old-school salons. What was he thinking? I hadn't done a roller set since school and was not fond of perms. That was the kind of hair you did in small towns, wasn't it? Kenny drove me by the place just three blocks from our home, right on Main Street across from the fire station and next to the post office. It had a For Sale sign in the yard. The location was great. I knew the three most important things in real estate: location, location, location. Could I really own my own saloon—I mean, salon? I never had any aspirations of being a salon owner, but I was willing to take a look at the place. I made the appointment. It was originally a single-family home but was converted into a duplex and had been used for several different small businesses over the years. No updates had been done in decades, but Kenny and I both had a vision.

We made a lowball offer, and it was accepted, to my surprise. It may have been the fact that the owners, a precious elderly couple, had known Kenny since he was knee high and he helped them from time to time with electrical work.

We closed on the soon-to-be salon in December of 2006 and gave the upstairs tenant until March to vacate. I quit my job at the end of the year, and Kenny installed a shampoo bowl in the basement of our home, so I could maintain the clientele who wanted to follow me all the way to Podunk, Lawton.

―⚉―

Kenny and I went to Florida for our honeymoon that January. I planned on it being a sober event. I really wanted it for us. I sucked Kenny into going to a tennis resort although Kenny had never played before. We played tennis for sixteen hours over four days. We were on different courts because of our different skill levels, but Kenny really enjoyed it. We even played some singles a couple of times after our lessons. Kenny was a great sport.

Our second evening there, we went out to dinner, and I *had* to have just one beer. I talked Kenny into having one too. There was far less guilt when Kenny drank too. Problem was, one was too many and a thousand was not enough, so the saying goes when it came to us alcoholic types. I had a second beer at the restaurant then picked up a bottle of wine at the store in the resort because they didn't sell beer. After I finished the bottle of wine back in our suite, I insisted we go to the resort bar just a stone's throw away, so I could drink more, beer preferably. I was also attempting to quit smoking at that time and wound up spending seven flippin' dollars on a pack at the bar. Every attempt to quit smoking was always ruined by alcohol.

I regret to say, Kenny did not go to the bar with me that night, and he was quite angry. Oh well! I didn't care. ("I don't care" was my all-time favorite saying.) The rest of our honeymoon I spent chasing the almighty buzz as soon as the tennis drills were over for the day. As we headed home, I threw away my remaining few cigarettes, and I also vowed not to drink, for a while anyway. I didn't make it two days before falling off the wagon again.

I began working on the salon plans when we returned. It was up to me to design and decorate, and that was a blast. A number of people over the years had asked me for advice on decorating and paint choices after seeing how I'd decorated my own homes. I also counseled many on furniture and art arranging. I'd never had any schooling in interior design, but of course, my friend Roxy told me I should look into it as a career. The problem for me was dealing with other people's tastes. Helping somebody decorate their country or traditional home would never satisfy me. I was a snob when it came to all that. I either loved something or not. There were no gray areas.

The salon was my opportunity to really shine. In March of 2007, we began the long process of remodeling. We started in the upstairs apartment, gutting the kitchen and bath, replacing carpet, and adding ceramic flooring. I quickly learned how to measure, cut, and install ceramic tile flooring. I really had fun using the wet saw, although my expertise was in the task of patching, caulking, prepping, priming, and painting walls. As long as the beers were flowing, I could do anything, even cut the hole for the new kitchen sink. We were both perfectionists, so we worked together beautifully and had this cool synergy. We completed the apartment in about four months and moved our tenant from the salon space to his brand-new apartment. He was thrilled to get out of the dump he'd been living in for six years. Our tenant was *movin' on up*!

The salon itself would be the big job. We gutted and gutted, tearing down old walls. We built new ones. The demo was the easy part, and very enjoyable. Kenny was shopping daily at Menards, bringing in loads of drywall and lumber. The labor involved was intense. I was spending eighty hours a week there, and Kenny was working his full-time job, plus an additional forty hours or so on the renovation.

Problem was, I was free to drink as much as I wanted now that I was no longer working, and things were getting way out of hand. Don brought over a *special* six-pack of beer for us that summer. *Atwater Hell* was the name. He must have been reading my mind.

It was in the midst of the salon remodel, July of 2007, when Kenny and I became members of the church. Pastor Mark was awesome, and I was craving his messages. When he asked Kenny and me at our first membership class why we wanted to become members, I blurted out, "Because we love you, Mark." I think he liked that answer. When we received the paperwork from our first membership class, I was not familiar with the line "I believe in Jesus Christ as my Lord and Savior," and I wanted to memorize it, but I kept getting the words screwed up. It sounded so foreign to me, but I was willing to learn. I was feeling the need.

Kenny put a lot of pressure on me to back off the tennis so we could get the salon open for business, but tennis was one of the only positive outlets in my life. I was playing eight to ten hours a week. He didn't realize that tennis was keeping me from hitting rock bottom. The amount of alcohol I was consuming skyrocketed. Now I was drinking from the time I woke up. I didn't have tennis to abstain for anymore, and instead of waiting to drink between noon and three o'clock, I was indulging when I woke up and made sure I had a case of beer at the salon to get me through the day.

It wasn't long before I started having frequent puking episodes and dry heaves in the morning, choking down the first couple of beers until I finally leveled off and could continue drinking for the rest of the day. It had been a long time since I could even brush my tongue; the gag reflex was always lurking. For the first time in my life, I had the shakes until I drank a couple. I forced down protein shakes when I could but had many failed attempts. I ate as little as possible because I didn't want to ruin my buzz, and I couldn't stand that feeling of being full. The liquid bowels were outrageous, and I was suffering from heartburn and chest pains.

Kenny was becoming more concerned. I had visited the emergency room twice in the past for chest pains. Once at age twenty-seven and once while pregnant with Aubrey. The chest pains were more severe than ever, so I called Kenny at work and told him I was going to the emergency room. It felt as if someone was clenching my heart, and I was having difficulty breathing. I was sure they would find something. I had the works, EKG and a stress test on the treadmill, and *again*, they found nothing but a couple of spots on my lungs which I was told were not unusual.

I was exhibiting signs that my condition was deteriorating. I was never a bed-wetter like some of the drunks I knew, but I had an incident in the middle of the night. Instead of getting up and going to the bathroom just a few steps away, I got up, opened the nightstand drawer, and proceeded to pee. Kenny woke up to his horror and questioned what I was doing. I was completely wasted; what a mess. That was a pretty low moment, especially with Kenny catching me in the act. I was so embarrassed.

I was isolating myself even more. Kenny was clueless about the amount I was drinking and the occasional cocaine and meth use. I hid it well. I was a master of deception. I even stooped as low as to smoke meth with a girlfriend in our master bathroom while Kenny was hanging out on the deck.

Kenny began making frustrated comments to me like, "So, are you going to drink your dinner again tonight?" This went on for a couple months. Kenny was sick of me reeking of alcohol every day when he came home from work, and so he distanced himself. I couldn't blame him, but this was when I needed him the most. I suppose I needed to be a little more broken before God could use me.

Most often, I was not noticeably drunk, how you might picture an alcoholic. I was highly functional, a professional, and that fact really messed with my head. How could it be wrong when I had this gift of managing my buzz at such a high level? My thinking was obviously extremely twisted. It was tough work mentally to maintain control. I was completely burned out on my lifestyle, like working two full-time jobs. Miraculously, I made it through the summer. I often thought I should leave Kenny to put *him* out of his misery. I couldn't stop on my own, and Kenny was not equipped to help me. He couldn't wrap his brain around my condition.

My life was going down the toilet fast, so I made a plan. As soon as Aubrey was back in school that fall, I was going to get an education on what I had become. I chose rehab. I knew I had a problem. I'd known for years, but it was damn hard to admit it to someone else. I was not willing to "screw this one up," as my dad put it. Rehab was something I should have done decades before on my own. I never wanted my addictions to become somebody else's problem, but it was too late. I wanted Kenny to be my hero, but it was going to take more than his love. I could only imagine the relief Kenny must have felt when I uttered the words, "I want to go to rehab." He was highly supportive of my decision, you think?

NOT CELEBRITY REHAB

I reported to rehab on September 10, 2007, before our first wedding anniversary. I drank only fifteen beers the night before—trust me, I counted—with plans of them being my last. Entering rehab felt like chopping off my right arm, mourning the death of a loved one and having my very best friend turn on me, all at the same time. What could life possibly be like without drugs and alcohol? I had been under the influence of mood-altering substances for over thirty years. How would I cope and would I even like myself? Who was I anyway?

I gave Kenny my one-y, which I'd had for twenty years now. That was like handing over my Pooh Bear. He disposed of it that night, and I showed up to rehab sober, unlike many people, I soon learned. They tested my blood, and all they found was marijuana. I was looking to give up cigarettes as well. I wanted to quit it all and just get it over with. I actually told my daughter I was going away to stop smoking, not knowing that they highly recommended not even attempting to give up the cigarettes for a year. I had been smoking for over thirty years too, and was *dying* to stop.

I was in detox for two days, with no symptoms of withdrawals. I learned that alcohol withdrawals were the only ones that could kill you and you should not attempt to quit on your own.

I took *The Book of Awakening* by Mark Nepo, which Mom had given me years before, inscribed, "Amy, to help you discover all that is you. Thanks for all the joy you bring, Mom and Dad." I also brought crossword puzzle books, which I did routinely before bed—yes, after drinking a case—and a head shot of Kenny lying on the beach. They also allowed me to bring my hair tools, which I was shocked and thrilled about.

I spent the first day in bed, sobbing nonstop. It was the most humbling experience of my life, and although I knew I was doing the right thing for a change, I was in the depths of self-hatred, but not pity. I owned it. I allowed this monster to dwell inside me. I just wasn't sure if I could break free from the chains of bondage. My greatest fear was not being able to get better; maybe I'd discover I was a lost cause. Whatever the outcome, I was going to take full advantage of what rehab had to offer.

While in detox, I was not required to attend any classes or meetings, but on the second day, I got up, cleaned up, and dressed up to face my harsh reality. There was a separate smoking room for those in detox, and the first person I met was a seventeen-year-old girl. I asked her what she was in for, and she responded, "Heroin." I thought to myself, *Oh, Lord.*

Her parents had sent her, but she wanted out. She told me how her girlfriend got her hooked. This wonderful friend of hers started whoring her to her heroin dealer as a means of payment. The girlfriend came into detox the next day, and she had an escape plan. Five days later, these two young girls were picked up by the dealer and were using again before they left the parking lot. How tragic!

I graduated to residential on the third day and was feeling pretty strong. I was a student of addiction now, on a mission to glean what I could while there. I socialized as much as possible, and it felt a bit odd without a beer in hand, the great social lubricant. I discovered that most of the residents were not there voluntarily, and some had been in before, four or five times or more. The most common addiction was the opiates: heroin, Vicodin, and OxyContin. Cocaine, meth, and alcohol were close seconds. Nobody was in for marijuana addiction, although I firmly believed it was a *gateway* drug. It can lower inhibition, so experimenting with other drugs was more likely. Dope could take away ambition and make you lazy and hungry too. I'd never bought into the concept of medical marijuana being prescribed and couldn't believe it was helpful in many areas. I had personally heard of the medical marijuana law being easily abused. I would bet a lot of money that the majority of my fellow rehabbers first smoked a little weed before graduating to the drugs that landed them in rehab.

My heart went out to my kindred, and I could tell that most of them would not make it through. They weren't in for the right reasons, and most of their circumstances would not support their recovery when they left. Many had lost everything due to their addictions, and their only option after getting out was returning to the dysfunction at home, missions, halfway houses, or the streets where drugs were prevalent. In other words, most returned to the hellholes they came from. I didn't know why, but my rock bottom wasn't nearly as low as the majority of those in the rehab with me. I still had the ability to count my blessings.

One young man from rehab stood out in my mind. He was a heroin addict and a cutter, twenty-two years old, and gay. This precious boy privately showed me the massive number of scars up and down his legs and arms. I'd never seen anything like *that*. The poor lost soul managed to pull a blade out of a disposable razor and cut himself in a bathroom stall while there, in rehab. Another young man noticed the blood dripping on the floor and stopped him and cleaned up his mess, and nobody said a word to the staff. This poor young heroin addict introduced me to his mother and his sister on Family Night, and I could see and feel his mother's immense pain. I wasn't sure if he even graduated. I left before his time was up.

This was what he wrote on the Peer Feedback sheet he gave me the day I was released. "I've talked with you more than any other woman here. You have been so nice to me, caring, and loving. You've been telling me I don't need drugs. I love you, and I think of you like a sister, from another mister."

The person that I connected with the most was an alcoholic woman in her mid-fifties. She looked almost out of place. She recently went through a divorce after thirty years of marriage. She was blindsided by her husband's decision. Never being a drinker prior to the divorce, she chose alcohol to help ease the pain. Four of her best friends packed her bags and brought her to this facility out of fear for her life. She turned alcoholic seemingly overnight, and she could not deny it or explain why she couldn't quit drinking. We both felt like we could beat this thing and spent our time together commiserating. I tried to show love to all the residents. I *so* got their pain and suffering. I cried a lot of tears for many of my peers while I was there.

Family Night was the only time I was allowed to see Kenny. Family and friends could come and attend an Al-Anon meeting and visit for a half hour afterward. Al-Anon is a program for the family and loved ones of addicts. It's a great educational tool and support system.

We were allowed to use a pay phone while in residential, and I talked to Kenny every night. I phoned my parents once too. That was really awkward.

The schedule was busy, but I made time to give haircuts free of charge. One young meth addict was so thankful he tried to pay me with laundry detergent. The thought was really sweet!

This was not a lockdown facility. They wouldn't stop you from walking out, and sadly enough, many did. People were kicked out for using as well. The center did so-called random blood tests. A cocaine addict asked me to style her hair in the bathroom before classes started one morning. Her pupils were blown up, and she had noticeable tics; it takes one to know one. I questioned her, and she denied using, but happened to be plucked out in the middle of a class that day. Rumor was, her own father brought her cocaine on Family Night.

The drama was never ending, with forty or so dysfunctional addicts all jonesing for their drug of choice. Tempers flared, and the staff had to be on their toes. I kept my focus and got the education I was looking for. I was incredibly relieved they stressed seeking a higher power. I was all about that because I'd proven I did not have the strength to get sober *on my own*.

I purged as much as I could while in rehab. I took this very important opportunity to share in a class called "Life Stories," before a large group, about Angel and the effect she'd had on my life. It was difficult and gut-wrenching, but necessary. I cried so hard I got the "zup-zups," an indication of intensity. This was the very first time I shared the entire Angel story. I never thought it made any sense to bring it all up again. I hated to bother anyone with my issues. I was an upper, darn it! It was something I should have done a whole lot sooner. I could feel my burden lighten. The healing had begun. They really stressed journaling as well, but I straight-up refused. I hated writing, and I couldn't type.

Everyone was asked to memorize the Serenity Prayer. "God, grant me the serenity to accept the things I cannot change, courage to change the things I can, and the wisdom to know the difference." I spent a lot of time contemplating those words. I graduated on day eleven. Fewer than 50 percent of the residents graduated by my calculations (I made a list of all the residents coming and going while I was there). Those were some pretty grim numbers. Not to mention the recidivism rate. Far too many would return to rehab.

Kenny picked me up, and we were off to my first official AA (Alcoholics Anonymous) meeting. I was astonished to discover how large the meeting was, with about thirty people in attendance. I was becoming acutely aware of the extent of this alcoholism and addiction issue, and I was far from alone. One thing for sure, alcoholism did not discriminate. These were people from all walks of life, in all age ranges.

At the beginning of the hour-long meeting, they asked if it was anybody's first time, so I raised my hand. A half-dozen people and I went into a separate room for my initiation, as it were. They went around the table and told me their stories, and in the last few minutes, I shared a little of mine. They made me feel very comfortable. At the end, we joined the others, stood in a circle, held hands, and said the Lord's Prayer, which was customary after every meeting.

> Our Father who art in Heaven, hallowed be Thy name; Thy Kingdom come; Thy will be done on earth as it is in Heaven. Give us this day our daily bread; and forgive us our trespasses as we forgive those who trespass against us; and lead us not into temptation but deliver us from evil. For Thine is the kingdom the power and the glory forever and ever. Amen. (Matthew 6:9–13 NKJV)

It was pretty cool. I still had it memorized from childhood. For the first time I attempted to find the meaning of this prayer.

REBIRTHING

My sobriety took priority over everything else including the salon remodel and playing tennis. I was fitting in an AA meeting every single day. I learned some horrible truths in rehab and AA. There was only one thing I needed to change to stay sober, and that was *everything*. That's exactly what I was beginning to do, and not living in the Zoo was a big plus. I cut off a handful of friends or, should I say, drug contacts.

Roxy and Lauren were another issue. I loved my girlfriends and had to inform them that I could no longer partake in the things we had enjoyed together for so many years. They were extremely supportive and would abstain while in my presence because they loved me. But honestly, they were triggers. Hell, life was a trigger for that matter. Everything I did and everywhere I went, once revolved around a party of sorts.

Church was a safe place, but I knew almost nothing about religion. I never cared before. I'd been too busy being an extreme party girl. I used to run from Bible thumpers. They were just a bunch of weirdoes. Come on—get a life!

I had to lay down my pride and admit I needed God's help for the first time. I would recommend it to everyone. I had a lot of questions, though. Could Jesus really be the Messiah? I had been exposed to too many conflicting and confusing ideas over the years. I was again looking for answers. I wanted to believe. I mean, really, what did I have to lose? Kenny was a true believer and an amazing person. He was reading Charles Stanley's *Life Principles Daily Bible*. I had opened a few Bibles over the years, but I guess you could say my heart wasn't in it. I started reading Kenny's Bible and *it* was different. I told Kenny how much I was enjoying it, and the next thing I knew, he'd bought me my very own copy. It was broken down into daily readings and included "Life Lessons" and other input from Charles Stanley. It was a beautiful thing.

One Sunday, Pastor Mark mentioned a book at the end of his message that he highly recommended, *The Case for Christ* by Lee Strobel, for loved ones who had doubts and questions. It sounded like a good book for me. I stepped foot inside the Christian Family Bookstore for the first time and purchased it. This book explained many things that I was curious about and it was very interesting to me that the author set out to discredit Jesus and in the process of his research became a born-again believer.

I had completed about sixty AA meetings in sixty days now, and we were at the end reciting the Lord's Prayer. When we got to the part that said, "Your kingdom come, your will be done," the words swiftly penetrated my softening heart. It was at that very moment that it finally sank in. It was not about me. It was about *God's will* for my life. As I contemplated the crucifixion, the most incredible example of love and sacrifice the world had ever known, I completely grasped the significance and power of what took place on Calvary. That was my moment of clarity, that was when I was born-again, and my life would never be the same. I could not take God's gift for granted. It was time to take the focus off of me and ask God what I could do for him. *What is your will for my life? What would you have me do?* My will had made a mess of me.

I'd walked around my entire life giving God the bird, so to speak, with all my drinking and drugging. I knew now that all those years of partying were a sin. When I got home, I started praying, really praying for the first time. On the floor with my head hanging down, face in my hands, I began weeping uncontrollably. I apologized for all my transgressions, begging for forgiveness. The fact that God loved me despite my thirty years of rebellion against him blew my mind and brought me to my knees. I could never use drugs or alcohol again without a great deal of angst.

Addiction was a completely selfish affliction. From the moment I woke in the morning, until I went to sleep at night, all that really mattered was the almighty buzz. I always knew how many beers were in the fridge and how low I was getting on cigarettes and dope. These thoughts were all consuming. I worshiped drugs and alcohol. I was suffering from extreme soul sickness. All I could do now was to attempt to live a life that was pleasing to God.

My thought patterns began to change, and it was as if the clouds had been lifted after I had finally admitted that my past was full of sin. I'd never thought of my life as sinful before. All I could do was repent, repent, and repent as I recalled the things I had done and what I had become. And when I surrendered, I left it all at the foot of the cross. Intensely humbling yet necessary, this was my first step toward ultimate recovery. The cure for addiction was not about behavioral modification or going to meetings; it was about seeking a personal relationship with God. The thing was, God had been waiting for me. He would not come into my life forcefully, but he did when he felt there was an opening. This was a matter of my softening heart. God was patiently waiting for all of us to call out to him.

I knew I had been forgiven. Tears well up in my eyes every time I think about how merciful God is and what a wretch I am. I was saved by grace through faith and nothing else. Just like the words of my dad's favorite song, *Amazing Grace*.

> How precious did that Grace appear
> The hour I first believed…

That's when it happened: the hour when I first believed.

I was a brand-new creation, and the changes in me were not yet visible, but I could feel it. I did not have to see to believe. This book about Jesus, the Bible, was the tangible proof I needed. God made it so simple for us by sending his son to die on the cross for the forgiveness of our sins. What happened to me that day was very profound, yet amazingly simple. I believed.

PURE LOVE

I had heard it said that the first year of marriage was the hardest. I had to agree with that statement in our case. I was born-again in November, 2007, at age forty-two, just after our first anniversary. Kenny adored me and, for our anniversary, gave me a framed photo of us standing in front of the World Globe taken from Arthur Ashe Stadium when we went to the 2006 US Open in New York. Etched on the glass was 1 Corinthians 13:7: "Love: It always protects, always trusts, always hopes, always perseveres." He was not giving up on me! What a comfort.

Kenny and I had talked about getting tattoos when we met. Neither one of us ever had one, so we decided to take the plunge. We didn't know what we wanted, but the tattoo parlor we went to had thousands to choose from. Kenny picked a cross. I liked that idea, but continued to browse. I'd know it when I saw it, and I did. I came across the word *faith*, and that was that. I had it tattooed on my lower back.

My Grandma Oberski gave me a mustard seed necklace for my first communion. It had no significance to me at age ten, but it sure did now. Jesus said, "I tell you the truth, if you have faith as small as a mustard seed, you can say to this mountain, 'Move from here to there' and it will move. Nothing will be impossible for you" (Matthew 17:20). Faith was exactly what I was all about now. I believed I could move my mountain. The tattoo was perfect.

Continuing to grow in my faith, I decided to check out Christian music radio and instantly fell in love with the focus on God. The opposite of garbage in, garbage out; it was time to fill my free time with light. I was ready to receive anything that could bring me closer to God. I'd been living in the dark for so long. This was where it was at. No more secular radio for me if I could help it. I turned Kenny on to Christian radio, and he fell in love too. Why hadn't we picked up on it sooner? The music and the DJs were filled with a spirit of hope and encouragement, two of the things I needed to stay the course.

My immediate family knew of my plans to go to rehab. I followed up with them when I got out, searching for love and support from those closest to my heart. Like everyone else, my family was unaware of the severity of my problem.

My brother Christopher and his wife came to visit that Christmas after rehab. Sissy told me it was their way of showing support. Christopher and I had a special connection as young children. He had always been so intelligent. As a child, I thought of him as Spock from *Star Trek*, our favorite show when we were growing up. He showed little emotion as a teen, and it was not logical for him to experiment with drugs and alcohol.

He never had a drink, smoked anything, or tried illicit drugs. We were polar opposites, it seemed. He was the oldest, and I was the youngest. He had a doctorate in artificial intelligence, a master's in computer science, and a bachelor's in physics, and I was a high school dropout. He was a bookworm, and I was an extreme party girl. He lived a clean and sane life, and I lived a dark and crazy one. Nevertheless, one thing we did have in common was our love for one another, and nothing could change that.

My sister Sissy was as sweet as always and sent several cards of encouragement and cheer. She was proud of me for facing my giants and she was a close second to Christopher with regard to mood-altering substances. Even after all the years of being figuratively beaten over the head with the Bible by her husband, Sissy still professed Jesus Christ to be her Lord and Savior. She was the only one in my family at that time that I could really discuss my newfound faith with.

I also called Angel. She was on her third marriage and living down South. Her second marriage had ended badly, and she left Michigan before her ex found some way to ruin her teaching career. She had joint custody of their young son but was spending extended periods of time away from him due to her move.

Angel was still struggling with depression as well as being recently diagnosed with fibromyalgia and she had been on various medications for many years. When I spoke to her that day, she confessed to me that she'd taken herself to the doctor after cutting her wrists. She was suicidal again. Over the years, she had shared with me many times her thoughts about ending her life, but she'd never told me about an actual attempt. Being away from her son and having to deal with her ex was taking its toll on her, I guess. She was weeping and had not told her husband, who was out of town at the time, about what she had done.

I wasn't sure what to do, so I pulled something out of my *AA Big Book*, hoping it would make her feel better. Having a long-distance relationship with her was scary for me. I used to be able to console her face-to-face. I worried about her often. What I read to her was something I really had to get a grip on myself, having read it several times since rehab. I didn't know, but maybe it would help.

> Acceptance: and acceptance is the answer to all my problems today. When I am disturbed, it is because I find some person, place, thing or situation–some fact in my life–unacceptable to me, and I can find no serenity until I accept that person, place, thing, or situation exactly the way it is supposed to be at that moment. Nothing, absolutely nothing, happens in God's world by mistake. Until I could accept my alcoholism, I could not stay sober; unless I accept life completely on life's terms, I cannot be happy. I need to concentrate not so much on what needs to be changed in the world as on what needs to be changed in me and my attitudes.
>
> —*AA Big Book*

It may not have been the most appropriate thing, but I knew she'd get it. I mailed her a bunch of other things I'd picked up at rehab and AA with a card of encouragement. Not a day goes by that I don't say a prayer for Angel.

My brother Danny never really expressed his feelings about my situation, but I'm certain he had spent some time reflecting on my demise, which I considered a good thing.

Of course, I kept Mom and Dad up-to-date. They were very proud of me and were fully aware of my conversion. Unfortunately, they didn't seem all that crazy about the fact that I described myself as a Jesus freak now. It's very difficult to explain it to someone who hasn't had a similar experience. They had been there, done that in relation to religion, and came across hardhearted. Mom and Dad had studied world religion and new age spirituality after leaving the Catholic Church. Even so, Dad said I was never going to change his religion, and he would die a Roman Catholic. Mom, on the other hand, was still searching for answers. I just wondered why they were so defensive.

BACKSLIDING

I completed the ninety meetings in ninety days after rehab and remained sober the entire time, but little did I know that I was in for the battle of my life. The devil had different plans for me, and he was not going to give up that easily. I was not prepared for Satan, who was indeed the author of confusion.

I made it from September 10, 2007 to New Year's Eve sober. Kenny and I decided to play some blackjack at a nearby casino that New Year's Eve, and I felt the need to have a beer while gambling. This was what they called stinkin' thinkin' in AA. No harm done, right? It was the beginning of my first relapse. I reassured Kenny that I had it under control. A couple of days later, I had a couple more beers, and before I knew it, I was drinking way too much again. I was a Christian in the middle of a relapse.

I was still reading my Bible, going to church, and listening to Christian radio. I was in what seemed to be a constant state of prayer, trying to figure out why I relapsed. I didn't give up hope, and drinking and drugging were a more painful proposition than ever. I never left home without the new travel mug Kenny purchased for me. I kept it topped off with beer no matter where I was. On the mug was the word *grace* in large letters, followed by the scripture; For the Lord God is our light and protection. He gives us grace and glory (Psalm 84:11). My thinking was so distorted.

Sadly, I convinced myself that I could use another one-y and had Roxy pick one up for me in the town where she worked. She questioned me, but I was in control, and what I wanted, when it came to my buzz, I could get. It was awful that I put her in that position. Roxy did not like doing it, but I used my powers of persuasion.

I planned a solo trip to Las Vegas to attend a hair show and visit my parents for a few days in late January. I had to break the news to Mom and Dad that my visit would not be a sober event. When I told them over the phone, my dad said, "So you found Jesus, huh?" I responded, "Actually, Jesus found me," and then changed the subject. The comment really hurt. All I knew was that I was a born-again Christian and relapsed. I had a new heart, but it didn't mean I was perfect. This was a process I was going through, and I continued to pray for God's will in my life. I suppose I wasn't buying into the fact that I could never use again even though controlled drinking was impossible. I had proved that time and time again.

Kenny had an iPod that I had no interest in. I struggled with technology illiteracy, but he loaded it up with music and a couple of podcasts for me to take on the trip anyway. Kenny discovered Greg Laurie's radio broadcast and checked him out online. We'd also started receiving Greg's *Daily Devotions* sent to our e-mail. We fell in love with this guy. Ironically, I listened to my first two podcast sermons while in Sin City. I enjoyed the messages and listened to them more than once. I also fell in love with Damita's song "Truth," with TobyMac and Mandisa's song "Shackles." They were two of my favorite songs now. I listened to these two songs dozens of times while on the trip.

My daughter, Aubrey, and I really started getting into some TobyMac. Aubrey's favorite song on the radio was "Made to Love." We purchased the *Portable Sounds* CD at the Christian Family Bookstore. After I listened to it a few times, I wound up purchasing it for Angel and had it express-mailed to her down South, hoping she would find it uplifting. I'm not sure why, but a little while later, I felt the need to send it to my brother Christopher, as well.

Although I was drinking again, I returned from Las Vegas with a burning desire to tap into more podcast sermons, thanks to Greg Laurie. Kenny found them, and we listened. Over the course of the next year and a half of my mind bending and relapsing, I listened to four or five dozen sermons a week.

———

While Kenny and I worked hard on the salon, we had our Christian radio cranked up. My favorite station, 91.3 WCSG, in Grand Rapids, Michigan, was often full of static at the salon, so I was searching for a different station and happened upon 92.1 Pulse FM out of South Bend, Indiana. I never knew it existed until that moment. Kimberly Ann Bonds, the Pulse

FM afternoon DJ was on, and it was so obvious she was spirit filled. I started listening to her every day. Her daily devotions stirred my soul, and most days, I burst into tears. Kimberly Ann was ministering to me and countless others.

I was listening to Pulse FM at home alone one day, and a different DJ posed a question to the listening audience. "A young addict had gone to Christian rehab camp and professed her faith in Jesus Christ. She relapsed sometime after getting out. Was she truly saved?" the DJ asked. I certainly could not speak for her, but I felt the urge to comment, so I called in, which was entirely out of character for me.

My response was aired on the radio. I explained that I was an alcoholic and drug addict and was in the midst of a relapse after being born-again. As painful as it was, it did not make me any less saved. The DJ didn't seem to be buying into the idea of using after being saved. His tone was skeptical. I hoped he was just playing devil's advocate, or maybe he didn't think it was possible. If it hadn't happened to him, how would he know? I was speaking from experience. Satan was still putting up a fight, and it was not difficult for me to find an excuse to backslide.

And backslide I did when my cat Tommy passed away. A gal I worked with back at the print shop when I was married to my first husband, Timothy, gave me Tommy when he was about a year old. He was the most lovable yellow tiger you could imagine; the type of cat that greeted everyone at the door, and if you pet him, you had a friend for life. He was a rock to me through my many trials and tribulations over the course of eighteen years. Unconditional love, so difficult to find in a human being, made Tommy so very dear to me. He was an indoor kitty and required few visits to the vet, but he began having difficulty breathing. The only thing he'd been treated for over the years were the zits on his chin. Tommy took after me, Mom. We made a visit to the vet that day, and Tommy got a quick exam. The vet broke the news that Tommy had a cancerous tumor in his throat, and his time was very near. I was in disbelief and wanted to see the proof and requested x-rays. I was in denial.

I knew he was just a cat, but he was *my* cat and a source of light in my life. The vet told me she could put him down right then, or I could take him home. He might make it another week. I brought him home and loved him up for a couple of days, but the time had come. In the morning he was gasping for air. I begged Kenny to return home from work. I could not take Tommy to the vet alone. I was in no condition to drive, unable to see through the tears. I was devastated and started drinking early that morning, and the binge went on for days. Returning home without Tommy's warm welcoming that March of 2008 after all those years was all that I could bear. That odd feeling of something missing went on for months.

Mourning the death of my cat and on a beer run to Halftime, our local party store, I inquired about a collection jar next to the register. The woman at the register explained to me the unfortunate circumstance involving her relative that recently passed away. A thirty-four-year-old woman was found dead in her apartment along with fourteen empty Schnapps bottles. The woman at the register said she suffered from sclerosis of the liver, and all attempts to quit drinking failed, and she drank herself to death. This news hit me like a ton of bricks. I put money in the jar and left the store sobbing. I had a perfect view of the deceased's apartment from my salon; a sad and frequent reminder. I think God was trying to get my attention.

The grand opening of the salon was May 27, 2008, after a solid year of remodeling. I enjoyed my flexible schedule. I hung one of my father's small crucifixes prominently near the entrance and put a copy of *The Case for Christ* in the waiting area. (I bought six copies and gave five away.) I was hearing some amazing faith stories from many of my clients. One story came from a recovering meth addict who recognized the necklace I was wearing which happened to be the coin I received when graduating from rehab. On the front it read, *"To Thine Own Self be True. Unity, Service, Recovery,"* and the back has the Serenity Prayer. He had been to rehab a number of times and suffered from PTSD (post-traumatic stress disorder), as well as other addictions, but he loved the Lord. He enjoyed mission trips and going on prayer walks with his church. It was so cool that he felt comfortable sharing his story with me. The salon was a blessing, a gift from God in an odd way. This project was what finally caused me to hit bottom. I had Kenny to thank for that because I never cared to own my own business.

Now that the salon was open I was back on my beloved tennis travel team, after taking an entire year off. Struggling with my demons, I chose to have a couple of beers before one of my matches. I threw two cans in my tennis bag from the stash in my car. I sucked them down in the locker room right before I walked onto the court to face my opponent. I was playing number 1 singles, the spot I preferred in the lineup. I was down in sets 1-6, 0-5 and down in the game 0-40 and on my second serve. If I missed my next serve, I would lose the match, and game over! I prayed to God not to let it end this way, and instead of double-faulting to lose the match, I came back and won seven straight games and the second set 7-5. Now, we had to play a ten point tie-breaker to decide the match. I did not steam roll my opponent, but took the tie-breaker 10-7. It was nuts! I never drank before a match again. I think Satan was tempting me with that win.

I drank heavily on our first so-called mission trip to help Sissy in Iowa. It was always a bit strange to drink around those who were familiar with my struggle, but it didn't stop me.

Kenny and I took a week off. Sissy had just purchased a home on a lease option and under the radar in preparation for leaving her husband. We got there and did our thing, making repairs and painting. She was fully aware of our capabilities, but honestly, my sister was more in need of emotional support. I wanted nothing more than for her to get out of her abusive marriage. She had left him numerous times before but she always returned because of his promises to change and her guilt of possibly destroying her two boys. Kenny and I labored the entire time and had a blast doing it—no payment necessary. It felt so amazing to be a real help to Sissy.

My new heart was enabling me to focus more on the needs of others. Kenny and I volunteered for Habitat for Humanity and various opportunities within our congregation. We were reaching out in all directions. I really stuck my neck out, and even taught third-grade Sunday school for a year with the goal of getting my daughter plugged-in. It was a real stretch for me in the midst of frequent relapses and being a baby born-again Christian.

I had several extended periods of sobriety. I enjoyed being sober more than having a buzz. I was making progress. My relationship with Jesus was sucking the fun out of partying. I knew coppin' a buzz was not God's will for my life and the guilt and shame was tormenting my soul. I was so torn between being sober and using.

ROLLING, ROLLING, ROLLING

Due to my relocation to Lawton, the weeks I had Aubrey, I was required to take her and pick her up from school each day, forty miles round-trip.

The county roads were less than desirable for safe travel in the winter months. Heavy drifting and white-out conditions were just a part of good old country living. Kenny's White Silverado, which was now my transportation, gave me a sense of security.

I got Aubrey to school safely, leaving plenty early because of the blizzard conditions this particular morning. It was nearing ten a.m. as I slowly made my way back into Lawton. About a mile from home and chugging up a hill, the truck began to fishtail out of control. I was not sure if I hit a patch of ice or maybe a snow drift. The visibility was pretty lousy. I spun across the oncoming lane and slammed into the embankment as the truck rolled on to the passenger side with a sudden jolt. The passenger window shattered. I was hanging by my seatbelt looking at the snow covered ground, mud and broken glass where my Aubrey was sitting not long ago.

It took me a moment to pull it together, and figure out what to do. I released my seat belt and got my feet on the ground. I had on only a sweatshirt, sweat pants and flip-flops with socks. I was not prepared for this. I located my phone and called Kenny who was working at a Target in Kalamazoo at the time. I was not hurt beyond some scrapes and bruises but I was sick about wrecking the "chariot." Kenny was on his way and now I had to figure out how to get out. It seems as though I was trapped. The automatic window opener on the driver side wasn't working, until I figured out that I had to turn the key in the ignition. I opened the window and what a relief. I was getting a little claustrophobic.

I used the steering wheel to pull myself up and out of the driver side window that was facing the sky. As I jumped out, a woman was cautiously approaching. She told me she was in fear of what she might find but had to check it out. What a brave woman. She was so thankful that I was all right.

She had parked up ahead in a driveway, leaving her four young children in the van because she could not ignore the wreckage. She allowed me to sit in the passenger seat of her van and keep warm until Kenny or the police arrived. She had already called 911. The State Trooper who arrived on the scene did not give me a ticket. That was awesome because I had not had a traffic violation since I totaled the second car when I was nineteen, some twenty-three years before. I found that miraculous considering my lifestyle.

I officially totaled vehicle number three so it was time to buy a new car. We purchased a snow covered Toyota Rav 4 a few weeks later.

The thing I missed most about the truck was a decal of little Calvin on his knees praying in front of a cross. It was one of the first things I noticed the night Kenny picked me up for our first date and for some reason it always brought me comfort. When I told Kenny that I missed little Calvin he surprised me with a new sticker for the Rav 4.

THE BATTLE

I had an awesome idea to host a family reunion the summer of 2009, and Mom and Dad would stay with us. I missed my parents and asked all of my siblings to pitch in for round-trip tickets, and we all planned accordingly.

This was the perfect opportunity to celebrate Sissy's fiftieth birthday, which was only a couple weeks away. Her divorce was nearly final, and I was floored when I saw her. She looked at least ten years younger compared to just a year ago. The signs of being emotionally battered and bruised were fading away. She was as light as a feather. Over the years, our phone conversations had been pain filled and disheartening, almost always ending on a sad note, but the Lord gave her strength and removed her shackles.

Sissy brought me a large cross necklace as a hostess gift for putting her up that week. Angel happened to bring me a pair of cross earrings. My sisters obviously knew where I was at, although Angel was still struggling with the whole Jesus-is-just-a-teacher/spiritual-guru thing, and it drove me crazy. I could always sense her unsteadiness as if she were standing on shifting sand.

My dad also took this rare opportunity while the family was all together to show us around Notre Dame's campus and see firsthand his artwork on display at St. Mary's. What a treat!

I may have mentioned my dad is a very talented artist. He actually painted frescos on the exterior of the O'Laughlin Auditorium on St. Mary's campus with Jean Charlot in 1956. Yep, frescos like Michelangelo did in the Sistine Chapel. So cool! They'd been recently restored, and Dad said they looked just like back in the day.

Also, in 1956 Sister Madeleva, the president of St. Mary's, purchased a large crucifix from my dad, and it still hung in Le Mans Hall. I never laid eyes on it before. I didn't even know it existed, and I cried as I studied it for the first time. I just couldn't think of a more worthy subject matter. The large crucifix that hung over our piano most of my life had been reproduced. A bronze replica of it was purchased in 2005 by Dr. Mooney, the new president of St. Mary's and Sister Agnes Anne Roberts. It was chosen to be boldly displayed in the atrium of the new Spes Unica academic building on St. Mary's campus.

The reflection room in the Spes Unica building was home to my dad's smaller crucifix creation. The original was done in bronze. I liked to touch the crucifixes as a child, and Dad let me hold the small one sometimes; it was a very heavy little piece. Dad made a mold and reproduced a very limited edition in ceramic.

Mom and Dad actually sent one of these crucifixes to President Obama shortly after he was elected in

2008. They were pleased that Obama was president. Back in Mississippi, my parents were warned by certain individuals not to pay the colored help too well, and the family business suffered because of their support for the civil rights workers who were helping to set up freedom schools. I am proud to say I was raised color-blind.

The trip to South Bend meant a great deal to my dad. Needless to say, Kenny and I thoroughly enjoyed the tour. I was extremely proud of Dad's art and he was assuredly worthy of my praise and, like so many artists, was underappreciated.

I did not drink for eleven weeks prior to the family reunion. I was learning to love the freedom of sobriety, and with every relapse, I could feel the growing pains, the anguish, and the consequences of not living in God's will. I felt as if I was slowly but surely being nailed to my own cross. The turmoil was intense as the battle between the forces of good and evil raged on in the depths of my soul, my very own, very personal Armageddon. How would this battle end? I prayed for the conclusion; whatever it would be, just let me be.

I was on the verge of drinking myself to death. Friday morning and the day of my family's departure, I had a private discussion with my parents about my pathetic condition and the difficulty I was having staying sober. I asked them to pray for my next attempt to quit drinking that coming Monday. I certainly wouldn't have thought of stopping on a weekend. Little did I know that I would have my last drink *ever* in the wee hours of the morning that Saturday.

I finally reached that fated moment, this battle for my soul; *My Armageddon*. God pulled me up out of the pit. I had a revelation just like I'd been praying for. My fight, my battle was over. I knew it from the moment God spoke those words to me, "write the book." Whatever the purpose, that was beside the point. I had been relieved, released, set free, delivered and redeemed.

Missing church had not entered my mind for many months until that Sunday after My Armageddon. It was okay this time because I somehow knew the content would speak directly to me, so I told Kenny as he left. Of course it would. God had my attention now, and I could not ignore his call.

The sermon series that Sunday was entitled The Great Eight, and the headline, "Not Guilty!" The series, based on Romans 8, included the following:

> There is therefore now no condemnation for those who are in Christ Jesus. For the law of the Spirit of life has set you free in Christ Jesus from the law of sin and death. For God has done what the law, weakened by the flesh, could not do. By sending his own Son in the likeness of sinful flesh and for the sin he condemned sin in the flesh, in order that the righteous requirement of the law might be fulfilled in us, who walk not according to the flesh but according to the Spirit. (Romans 8:1–4 NIV)

Wow!

> I do not understand what I do. For what I want to do I do not do, but what I hate I do. I know that nothing good lives in me, that is in my sinful nature. For I have the desire to do what is good, but I cannot carry it out. (Romans 7:15, 18 NIV)

Yep! That was me to a tee.

> For in my inner being I delight in God's law; but I see another law at work in the member of my body, waging war against the law of my mind and making me a prisoner of the law of sin at work within my members. What a wretched man I am! Who will rescue me from this body of death? (Romans 7:22–24 NIV)

Jesus!

> What shall we say, then? Shall we go on sinning so grace may increase? By no means! We died to sin; how can we live in it any longer? (Romans 6:1–2 NIV)

Amen! I couldn't.

Kenny returned from church completely blown away. There could not have been a more appropriate sermon that day. God was just confirming what happened on Saturday. *Yes, I'm listening!*

I phoned the church that Sunday afternoon to set up a meeting with Pastor Mark and Becky. I had to tell them what the Lord had done for me; how he delivered me from my addictions and told me to write the book.

I spoke with Becky, and we planned on Tuesday. I composed a letter to them because I knew I'd be too nervous to speak. I tend to get tongue-tied, but they would understand and not judge me. I was ever so tired of backsliding, and this was another huge step in the right direction:

> Dear Mark and Becky,
>
> I must humble myself before you now. I need all the support and prayer I can get, and you are part of the missing link. Giving you (Pastor Mark) that crucifix several months ago was a way of reaching out to show my appreciation for all you've done for me already. I really love you guys and this church. I would like to hug you both. Can we pray on our knees? There might be something to it. I wanted to do this since rehab but was too embarrassed.

Pastor Mark was out of town. It was God's plan. I would not have been able to express myself as well. One-on-one with Becky comprised two of the most amazing hours of my life. I read to her an additional letter I wrote for the purpose of sharing not only with them but with those close to me. It summarized the recent events that took place and gave a brief overview of my life. I confessed my sins with no fear of judgment. I was now an open book. I didn't care who knew anymore. Becky said I was an apostle and God was using me all for his glory. It sure wasn't for mine. What I was about to do might not put me in a very positive light in some people's opinion, but it only mattered to me what God thought.

Becky showed me the video I missed from that Sunday's service: *The Source, Sealed—Part 1*. The video was made for me. I bawled as I watched it in her office, and when it was over, she asked if I would like to see part 2, which was not shown in church that day. Becky made the point of telling me that "the cool part is, you don't have to forgive yourself because you've already been forgiven." I finally got it, and this video was all about the nightmare I'd been living in and the freedom I'd found in Christ. The box in the video, where we kept track of all our mistakes and wrongdoings, only contained God now. Everything else was *sealed* in an envelope, never to harm us again. I let it all go. The video that Sunday was simply providential, there is no other way to put it.

Becky and I went to the sanctuary at the end of our meeting, knelt beneath the cross at my request while holding hands, and she prayed for me. Lord, that woman could pray. What a special gift. It was something to be admired, how freely the words flowed from her lips, so heartfelt and full of love and compassion. Her prayers had power. I could feel it; she exuded the Holy Spirit.

When I came home that afternoon, there was a message on the answering machine. Andy Krieger, our praise and worship leader, wanted to know if I would be interested in being a part of the coming Sunday's services. I returned his call immediately, and he explained to me that Becky shared with him my testimony of how God had been working in my life. Andy said this was the first time the church had ever done anything like this program entitled "Cardboard

Confessions." There was no way this was not God's plan. His timing was *sooo* perfect. He just continued to confirm what I was fully aware of. It is so humbling when you finally get a glimpse of God's awesomeness.

I stood onstage that Sunday with four other testimonies. We all held a piece of cardboard with our affliction written on the front and the result of God's work on the back. There was a breast cancer survivor, an amputee, a couple with a special-needs child, a woman who lost her father, and last but not least, me.

Mandisa's song "He is With You" played while different Bible verses showed on the big screen as our cue to, one at a time, reveal God's answer to our prayers. My cardboard said "Addiction," and as I flipped my piece, it said "Freedom" as "I will never leave you nor forsake you" (Hebrews 13:5) flashed across the screen. God would *never* let go of me. I knew that!

I was onstage for the nine a.m. and eleven a.m. services in front of over a thousand people. I trembled and wept some but kept my head held high. I was unbreakable! I invited Kenny's brother and sister, who happened to be clueless about everything, especially rehab. I was through hiding, and they were in for a big surprise. And, of course, I asked Lauren and Roxy to be there. I wanted their support. As a result, three of the four visitors that day started attending Southridge, praise God.

Out of the hundreds of people attending that morning, only a handful congratulated me in the lobby after the services. I think that proved there was quite a stigma attached to addiction. All the audience knew was that one word descriptive of me. That word alone was enough to scare people away. I was an addict. Let's face it; it was a dirty word. One of the individuals that dared to approach me was an eighty year old man I'd known for a couple of years from the YMCA. He said I was brave. Brave, maybe? Free? For sure!

I sent an e-mail on August 19 to Mars Hill Church in Seattle, Washington, for Pastor Mark Driscoll labeled "Must Read." I really wanted him to know what happened to me. I was seeking "wise counsel," as he put it, and I totally respected his preaching. His podcasts had helped me tremendously. He was highly gifted and had a great sense of humor. Pastor MD was a joy to listen to, especially when he went into rebuke mode. God bless him.

Kenny and I had been listening to the majority of his podcasts for over two years, and if we had to pick a favorite podcast pastor that would be difficult to do, but Pastor MD (Mark Driscoll) was definitely at the top of the heap. Funny thing was, when Kenny first discovered him while on the internet, I was peeking over his shoulder and told him that I'd blow by that one, but something intrigued my husband, and he started downloading. God bless *Kenny* for not always listening to me.

I was having a dialogue with Pastor MD for the first couple hours after I finished puking up my demons that morning. I was back on the chaise lounge, sizing up the magnitude of this endeavor I'd just begun. I wasn't sure how to go about writing a book, and I knew Pastor MD was published and was always working on a book. He was so well read; his personal library was beyond extensive. Who better to ask? Pastor MD would also fully understand what happened to me. God may not speak to everyone quite so clearly, but he certainly did to me, and Pastor MD could surely relate. I was chosen, and my purpose was to write a book to help save lost souls from alcohol and drug addiction. I needed help to accomplish my God-given mission, my orders from Heaven.

I was a bit dumbfounded at first, and I wasn't sure if I should close the salon to write full-time. What would I do when I had a manuscript? I was very concerned about computers. They scared me, but God said to write the book. Who was I to question God?

I stated in the e-mail how much Kenny and I loved him and his wife, Grace. I was not expecting a response from Pastor MD himself, knowing full well how extremely busy he was. I did receive a sweet note from a receptionist, and it was a real comfort for me to find out that Mars Hill Church was not impenetrable. Who knows? Maybe he did read my e-mail, I could dream. Regardless, Mars Hill was a mega church doing awesome kingdom work, and the response meant a lot to me.

While reading my *Life Principles Daily Bible* by Charles Stanley that evening as I routinely did, this scripture quote jumped out at me:

1 Corinthians 1:27: God has chosen the weak, despised, and "inconsequential" things, people, and events to demonstrate His majesty, so "...that the excellence of the power may be of God and not of us."(2 Corinthians 4:7)

It was as if God was speaking to me! He was using *me*. I read somewhere that there was no such thing as a coincidence. It was just God wanting to remain anonymous.

JUDGE NOT OR NOT?

Aubrey's best friend's mom was a drug counselor, and it just so happened she called on August 20 to set up a play date. I shared with her what happened, and she thought it was wonderful. She told me I'd be on *Oprah* one day with a story like mine. She thought it was great that I was into Jesus, but in her opinion, Jesus was not enough for sustained recovery. I did not tell her that I disagreed with that statement. It was a shame that most secular counselors didn't realize or acknowledge the power of Jesus. Even after my miraculous testimony, she could not open her mind to what I proclaimed. I was healed!

She did warn me of the chemical imbalance of the brain after long-term use of drugs and alcohol, and I could understand her line of thinking. She recommended I seek a doctor's advice. I had not slept in five days, and that concerned her. My doctor squeezed me in and wrote me a prescription for Librium and Trazodone. Maybe I could settle down now and get some sleep, not! Writing, writing, and writing.

Kenny and I had a wedding reception to attend on Saturday, August 22. Kenny's close friend's boy was getting married. I decided not to go with Kenny because physically, I was absolutely spent, but I quickly changed my mind when Kenny received the news that the day prior to the wedding his close friend's sister died in a motorcycle accident. I felt it was a sign that the Lord was calling me to go.

After the wedding I chose our spot at the reception. Champagne-filled flutes were at every seat. It was okay. I had thrown all the Antabuse away a week ago and did not have any cravings for alcohol, but I quickly gave my glass of champagne to a neighbor. I felt Satan lurking. I went out on the veranda to smoke a cigarette. I was using my handheld tape recorder because I didn't bring my pad of paper, and I was still on a roll. There was an older white-haired and bearded gentleman sitting alone off in the distance, staring at me. He reminded me of Santa Claus. I didn't think much of it.

Every one took their seats to pray before dinner. A very annoying woman next to me was texting throughout the entire prayer. That disturbed me!

As we were eating, I struck up a conversation with a woman at the table next to us. She happened to be the wife of Santa.

After dinner, I went back out on the veranda to have another smoke, and this couple was sitting together, so I asked if they would mind if I joined them. Santa made it clear he did not like my smoking but said okay. He asked his wife to leave, pulled a chair close to him and asked me to sit down. I told him that I noticed he was watching me earlier. Santa confirmed. He asked if I had been abused.

"Ah, yeah," I responded.

"Was it your dad?" he asked.

"Lord no," I told him. "I adore my father, but my sister abused me when I was young."

I wondered why he would ask me such a question, and I told him I was an alcoholic and quit drinking a week ago. Maybe that was the vibe he was picking up on? I wound up telling him about Angel and her fragile state of mind, the cigarette burns, the kicking and things. I told him that I struggled with my demons, and he laughed. He said, "Your sister has far more demons than you *ever* did."

I was aware of that. I'd been trying to get through to Angel for quite some time. I wanted to help her so desperately. The last time she lashed out at me was Memorial weekend at my place. A group of us were playing a game in the dining room, and Angel kicked me hard under the table. It came out of nowhere. I looked her square in the eyes and told her that if she ever did that again, I would kill her. I was not serious, of course. It brought back some horrible memories, but I was drinking heavily. It was nothing the almighty buzz couldn't take care of.

Santa performed a battery of tests with my fingers and a little piece of paper while mumbling some stuff, and then he gave me his business card. He was an acupuncturist. I had always been curious about acupuncture. I called that Monday and made an appointment. He told me he cast out demons a couple hundred times before, and he could help Angel, and I was interested in using acupuncture to quit smoking. I started to think that maybe Santa was a godsend.

Santa asked if I was taking any drugs, so I told him about the Librium and Trazodone. He became furious and described my doctor with all kinds of colorful expletives. He told me to throw those meds away and try sleeping with my Bible under my pillow. I slept like a baby from that night on with no need for drugs. I made it a habit for about three months. After reading my Bible at night I slipped it under my pillow. It was very comforting waking up in the middle of the night and wrapping my hands around it.

One night I forgot to put it under my pillow, and I had a nightmare. Angel was sitting very close to Kenny on a sofa with her arm around him. I grabbed her and threw her on the ground and was choking her. When I woke up, I realized I forgot to put my Bible under my pillow. My first thought was that Satan was attacking me while I was vulnerable. It was so strange that I even woke Kenny up to tell him. I put my Bible on *my chest* and went back to sleep.

I sent Angel a care package that included a letter full of advice to help her. I shared it with Santa on my second visit to give him a better idea of where I was coming from and where Angel was at. He said I needed to be careful and *not* to tell her Jesus was the only way. A red flag went up. Then he said he wouldn't touch most of the pastors I mentioned in the letter with a ten-foot pole. Another red flag! You didn't talk about my pastors that way. I made a judgment call and that was the last day I ever graced his place with my presence. He was definitely not what Angel needed, and I cancelled her appointment for the following week; so much for the exorcism.

MIGHTY VICTORY

After two months of sobriety, I attempted to quit smoking. Day two, I was very irritable. I liken the withdrawal symptoms to that of demon possession. I could have ripped all my hair out and ran around like a crazy person, screaming at the top of my lungs. I wanted the whole world to feel my pain.

Poor Kenny was not Johnny-on-the-spot that evening when I was ready to leave for my first Celebrate Recovery meeting (the Christian twelve-step version of AA). A hair client of mine invited me to check it out after I shared my testimony with her. Well, I picked a fight with Kenny on the way there and couldn't even focus on the meeting. On the way home, I demanded we stop at the gas station so I could pick up a pack of smokes. For whatever reason, it was not a good time to quit. Maybe God was just pleased that I was sober for two months. I really, really wanted to quit, but I didn't beat myself up about it like I used to. I'd try again at a later date.

—∽—

February 14, 2010, I was six months sober. And I did it! I quit smoking for good! I couldn't wait a year like they recommended in rehab. I prayed in preparation on a daily basis for four months that I could quit that February. I was very specific in my prayer. I wanted to quit without the demon-possessed type of withdrawals. I prayed to be mentally prepared and able to focus on all the positives of not smoking: clean lungs, more money, no more "stinky," and not being treated like a second-class citizen. But first and foremost, I finally had to admit that smoking was a sin and repent. If my body was a temple, smoking was the last thing I should be doing.

My quit date fell on a Sunday so I asked Becky to pray at the cross with me after the nine a.m. service. We knelt at the cross, and she asked me if I was going to do any kind of nicotine replacement. I chose to chew a 2 mg nicotine gum to help take the edge off, and I used it on and off for four months. I switched to straight gum and had no problems. In addition to the gum, I explained to Becky how I finally admitted that smoking was a sin and how I had been praying really, really hard. We held hands, and she did her thing again, leaving me speechless.

If you asked my husband or daughter how I was after I quit smoking this last time, they would tell you that I was as silly and happy as usual. I did not suffer from withdrawal symptoms, and I had averaged at least a pack a day for over thirty years. The love affair had ended.

I had to finally come to hate tobacco. All the years I fooled myself into thinking how hard it would be to quit and how much I enjoyed the taste, and the smell, and the way they relaxed me. That was a load of BS. I brainwashed myself because of the addictive quality. Yes, it's unfortunate that people smoke. I wish I'd have never started smoking. Cigarettes are extremely addictive. The tobacco companies make them that way. I heard in rehab that cigarettes have five of the same chemicals that are in today's meth, and it wouldn't surprise me in the least. I think most people are aware of what an epidemic meth addiction is. Like drug pushers and pharmaceutical companies, tobacco companies want to hook you hard. Money, money, money. I had to quit telling myself I couldn't quit and learn to despise cigarettes.

On top of the chemical element, there were many rituals that went along with cigarette smoking that increased the strong hold they had. I smoked with my morning coffee, after every meal, when drinking, and while driving. It was the first thing I did every morning and the last thing I'd do at night. It had just become so intertwined with daily life that when removed, there was a *gaping* hole. The hardest part for me this last time was while putting on my makeup. I was not having cravings, but I kept reaching and grabbing for that damned cigarette that didn't exist. It was deeply ingrained in my muscle memory; that was annoying. I overcame cocaine, methamphetamine, alcohol, and dope, but nothing compared to kickin' the cigarette habit. Months of prayerful preparation and conviction were the key for me.

While I was attempting to quit smoking several years ago, I remember Angel encouraging my efforts. With tears in her eyes, she told me she didn't want me to die of lung cancer, that she was supposed to die first because she was older. I found this very sweet. Angel was blessed to quit when she became pregnant at age eighteen. I was good and hooked by that age. She did have a very rare smoke when it suited her, usually when drinking. I also knew people that only smoked when they drank. I never could understand those darn part-time smokers.

I would advise those trying to quit to increase their physical activity and don't eat peanut M&Ms in bed! *I'm just sayin'*. I did gain about twenty pounds, but it was only temporary. After two years, I was back where I belonged, less than 130 lbs. I focused on being healthy, not thin, and have never felt better. The little bit of weight gain was the lesser of the evils. After thirty years of smoking, my body had to adjust to the new me. It was not necessary to gain tons of weight and I didn't feel that twenty pounds was too high of a price to pay to be nicotine free. Kenny happened to love my new curves, so he said. He was a wise, wise man.

I found it so appropriate that my six months of sobriety and the date I quit smoking fell on Valentine's Day. It really was a matter of the *heart*.

SERVE AND RETURN

I aspired to serve others after being born-again. I served not out of obligation or as a means to keep sober, but out of reverence. I did it in light of what Jesus had done for me. It was fascinating how naturally this happened. There was so much joy to be had when serving! My focus was on Jesus. It was all about Jesus. Once I started pursuing Jesus, something happened to me. I found a new capacity to love, and not only others, but myself.

Back in August, when I met with Becky, she highly recommended that I consider going on an upcoming mission trip. I told her to count on Kenny and me. In April 2010, we went on our first official mission trip to Annville, Kentucky, to minister to the Appalachians. Seventeen of us, Becky included, took two large vans and a U-Haul trailer to our destination, Jackson County Ministries. We spent four full days at work camp. Kenny and I were just made for this stuff; the dynamic duo. Kenny's electrical talents were put to use, and I was his apprentice, upgrading an electrical service to two hundred amps.

I helped Kenny rough in the wiring on a new three-bedroom, two-bathroom home in Lawton so I had some experience doing electrical work. I was climbing ladders, slamming holes in joists, and pulling wires from switch to fixture in no time. All the other trades on the job thought I was a for-real electrician. I must have looked like a natural in a tool belt. We also did a lot of ceiling dry wall on the mission trip, something else we were all too familiar with.

Our group was amazing, and the evenings were spent in fellowship and nightly devotionals. I signed up to do one of the nightly devotionals. It was a real stretch for me. I got so nervous when all the attention was on me. With sweaty palms and racing heart, I pushed myself outside of my comfort zone and shared with my brothers and sisters in Christ. I gave a brief personal background and read a rough draft of *My Armageddon*, then ended by reading out of my Charles Stanley Bible.

I'm certain I caught some people off guard with my testimony. There were elders and deacons on the trip and the responses I received were loving and sincere. The next day, an elder who was also a funeral director and a very pleasant gentleman, pulled me aside to thank me for sharing. He had a nephew who was on the verge of losing everything: wife, children, and home due to addiction. He was the last person there that I thought could relate to my story. Nobody was safe from the effects of drugs and alcohol.

After my devotional, a lovely lady who was very involved in the church pulled me aside to tell me that I'd be perfect for a new ministry she and two other women were in the process of starting up, *Wings of God Transition Home*. Their goal was to house and mentor women after incarceration and to share the gospel. She said I could talk turkey to these women from jail, and they wouldn't be able to pull the wool over my eyes. I took that as a compliment. I considered myself street-smart and I sure wasn't naive. I actually remembered hearing about the Wings of God Transition Home at a Forgotten Man Ministry dinner. She was there, and one of her partners spoke. I was intrigued by what they were trying to get going. God was in on this!

I did feel suited for jail ministry. My past had prepared me for it. If I could just get close enough to hug, listen, and share their pain. Planting seeds, that's what I could do with no fear of rejection. You can't win them all, but you don't know until you try.

A seasoned missionary on our trip volunteered for the devotional on our last evening in Kentucky. She had been on twenty-eight mission trips and in twelve different countries in the last eleven years and already had her next trip planned. How awesome to be called to serve so intensely. I knew if time and money allowed, Kenny and I would seek more opportunities to serve in this manner. It was not for everyone, but we couldn't wait to do it again, and we did return to Kentucky the following year.

For her devotional, she read a number of scriptures relating to service. It was what we were all called to do in many different capacities. Here are some of my favorites that she shared:

> The greatest among you will be your servant. (Matthew 23:11 NIV)

> I needed clothes and you clothed me, I was sick and you looked after me, I was in prison and you came to visit me. (Matthew 25:36 NIV)
>
> God is not unjust; he will not forget your work and the love you have shown him as you have helped his people and continue to help them. (Hebrews 6:10 NIV)
>
> Carry each other's burdens, and in this way you will fulfill the law of Christ. (Galatians 6:2 NIV)
>
> Each one should use the gifts he has received to serve others, faithfully. (1 Peter 4:10 NIV)

Before we left for home sweet home, we each received a Jackson County Ministry T-shirt. Their catch phrase: "DG4GS—Do Good For God's Sake! 2 Timothy 2:15."

Kenny and I returned from the trip more rejuvenated than if we'd spent a week on a tropical beach. This was the e-mail I sent our fellow campers when we returned:

> Dear campers,
>
> I have discovered in the past couple years that reaching out to help others in the midst of my struggles has been the best medicine. I received a healthy dose last week. Thank you all for lending your ear with love and compassion. As my family in Christ continues to grow, I will be seeking more opportunities to serve the least of these with arms wide open. Kenny and I have been blessed to share this last week's experience with all of you. Returning home has filled us with an overwhelming sense of gratitude. We have more

than we deserve. A trip such as ours has a way of putting life into perspective. I will strive to do a lot less whining.

Thank you, Jesus!

I attached it to Greg Laurie's *Weekend Devotion* that day. It was too perfect for me not to share: "Why Does God Allow Trials in Our Lives?" Greg starts out by saying, "God allows trials and hardship in your life so you can help others. As a result, whatever difficulty, challenge, or suffering you may be going through need not be wasted."

He makes three main points:

1. "There is no better time to minister to others than when you are hurting."

Don't sit around feeling sorry for yourself. Reaching out to others is great therapy!

2. "There is always someone worse off than you."

Amen to that statement. Focus on what you do have. "It could be worse" is one of my favorite sayings.

3. "Don't waste your experience."

Share your story! Someone may need to hear it.
I have forwarded dozens of Greg's *Daily Devotionals* to Angel. It's nice to share!

TOTALLY RANDOM

Becky suggested I bring along my haircutting tools to Kentucky, so I was looking for opportunities to use them. Across the lawn from our dorm was Barnabas Home for boys. These boys were wards of the state, ages fourteen to seventeen. Our paths crossed in the cafeteria so Kenny asked one of the state employees if I could offer free haircuts to the boys. I visited Barnabas Home after dinner and set up the schedule.

I had two evenings with about two hours each to spare. When the staff saw me set up on the front porch of our dorm, they started sending boys over one at a time. I plugged in my iPod player and cranked up some Skillet. A couple of the boys were familiar with and liked Skillet. I had quite the audience, and some of the work campers were crying and some took pictures. I touched eleven out of the thirteen young men staying in the home those two days.

I asked each boy why they were in and received various answers, from anger-management issues and drug and alcohol abuse, to "Dad's in jail" or "Mom's a drug addict." The first haircut I did was on the youngest boy. He was fourteen-years-old and a tiny boy wearing a cast on his arm. I asked how he broke it, fearing his answer. He said his father broke it sometime ago and never took him to the hospital to get it fixed. But because he was in this home, the state was fixing it. He was so excited about it, and was very thankful for his haircut.

One of the young men was quite confused about why some random woman from Michigan was cutting his hair. "This is random. You are random!" he kept saying. I agreed. Totally random! Another boy told me he was graduating in May and would be the very first young man to earn a high school diploma in his entire family. I'm not sure who was prouder, him or me. It touched me deeply because of my poor choices. I applaud any kid that made it through high school. The cards were definitely stacked against these boys.

Drew was a very sweet boy, and his story was unique. He told me that his mom sent him there to help him learn to be more independent. I noticed him the first day because he was wearing a T-shirt just like the sweatshirt I had brought with me. It had the words "Pray Hard" with a picture of someone wearing jeans with huge holes in the knees, and underneath the picture was, "1 Thessalonians 5:17."

Drew went to a church in Lexington, Kentucky, called Southland and had just been baptized along with many others while the sun was setting over a lake. He explained it as being "the most glorious experience of his life." He accepted Christ and, like me, wanted to spread the good news. He went on and on about Pastor Jon Weece and how amazing the church was. Drew said sixteen thousand people attended the Easter service that year and that I just *had* to listen to the *It* series.

It was so cool to see this kid on fire. Before he left, I made sure I wrote everything down, and I promised him that Kenny and I would check It out. One of the first things Kenny did when we arrived home was to download this *It* series, and it was everything this young man described to me and more. Another mega church and pastor doing amazing kingdom work by way of *radical love*. Thank you, Drew!

I served them as best I could. All I required was a great big hug after each haircut, and I didn't let anyone get away without one. I also made a point of telling each one I loved them.

You know, I think I probably could have handled some boys of my own although I wouldn't trade my daughter for the world. God bless all those boys!

I also found some time to cut several of the campers' hair and was very pleased that Frank, the guy in charge of the campers, took me up on a free haircut. He was a Canadian that went to Annville for a four-month mission trip and never left. He'd been there eleven years. He found his calling in Kentucky. I love the saying: "God doesn't call the qualified, he qualifies the called." I'm pretty sure that's how it happened for Frank. His efforts were making a difference, and his vision was great. Frank was a humble man of humble means.

PART 2
IT'S ALL ABOUT JESUS

GOT FAITH?

I made a career out of drug and alcohol abuse, spending thirty years of my life in this self-proclaimed profession. I figured I'd wind up being just another ugly statistic, dying prematurely of who knows what. So many people take their addictions to the grave; why would *I* be any different? I was about as lost as they get, right up there with the "best" of them. My past was frightening and a downright crying shame. By God's grace I came out the other side seemingly unscathed.

I felt I was beyond salvation, destined to live in this hell on earth, as I told Kenny when we fell in love. I made him promise to love me the way I was, but I wasn't aware of how deep his love was for me. Kenny loved me enough to rebuke me. He enjoyed the party girl in me for a minute, but eventually, his disapproval forced me to closely evaluate my life.

Nobody had called me on it before. He wasn't a control freak, just a man painfully in love with a party girl. This change in me that he was praying for was a mighty tall order. Kenny had nothing major in his life that needed changing, and it just didn't seem fair. Well, you know what? Life isn't fair.

I eventually came to the conclusion that I wanted to change, but I didn't know how. I was the one with the mountain to move, do or die; my choices, my consequences. Damn him for being right! I didn't know whether to love him or hate him sometimes. Kenny continued to love me somehow through it all, and our prayers were answered in God's time. There was a two year period I wished I hadn't had to go through, but who was I to question God?

I had to get right with God. That should be top priority for all of humanity. C. S. Lewis said, "The salvation of human souls is the real business of life." Amen! I am now making it my business. What else *really* matters? What an awesome gift to share. Kenny shared Jesus with me, and my life has been transformed.

I want to make this point for those of you who feel like giving up. Don't. You are playing right into Satan's hand. You must persevere. Be persistent, and pray like you have never prayed before. I know what it's like to feel like a piece of poop because you have picked up again. I know how hard it is to choose that new date to quit; only fearing failure and ridicule. God is listening. You must draw closer to him.

Please trust this old, die-hard party girl. Don't lose faith no matter how you feel. In the beginning, I still wasn't sure if it was God's will for me to stop drinking and drugging entirely. Today, I can tell you without a doubt that God's will is for us *not* to be a slave to anything of this world.

Now I am free. Free to love. Free to share. Free to serve. Free to encourage and give hope to the hopeless.

If you haven't hit rock bottom and are still toying with your stubborn pride, I will say it again: pride ultimately leads to destruction. Quitting is not a matter of willpower. It is a heart defect. If you are not ready to humble yourself and get down on your knees and admit that you are a sinner in need of God's saving grace, you will not reap the benefits. Where you need to go is not the easiest path. It is the path less traveled and the one that leads to the ultimate reward. Repentance is the beginning. We are all liars, thieves, and cheats. Apologize to God, and ask him for help.

The little Baptist church just a few blocks from my home posed a question on their road sign: "You can believe in God, but do you know him?" My answer is "yes." As soon as I started pursuing God, he began to reveal himself to me. This feeling of being filled with the Holy Spirit, happened to me. It may sound hokey, but it's the real deal. Now I know what true Christianity feels like and it's not about your denomination! And just showing up to church every Sunday doesn't count. It doesn't hurt maybe, but it doesn't count "Going to church doesn't make you a Christian any more than standing in a garage makes you a car!" I don't know who said that but I love it! Maybe you are just going through the motions?

If you are thinking about your next high, sexual escapade with someone other than your spouse, or a fast-food binge, your eyes are not on the prize. Ask yourself this question: If Jesus returned would he be pleased with what I am focused on? I now use that question as a gauge for my thoughts and actions. It helps keep me in check while I'm behind the wheel of a car or interacting with people, but most importantly, when I'm all alone and no one's looking and it's between just me and God.

And boy, was I dead wrong about those Bible thumpers. More like plain ignorant and hard-hearted. Now I understand why they couldn't help but want to share the good news. I have learned that I was never cool to begin with. I was delusional! But, "It's cool to be a Christian…" from the words of TobyMac and Kirk Franklin's song, *Throw Yo Hands Up*.

Unfortunately, these days, most people don't come to Christ until they've suffered a major crisis, like me. Most of us seem almost content living a mediocre life plagued with stress, addictions, and feelings of emptiness, uncertain of our purpose. We are created to love and glorify God. So simple, really, yet we will try just about anything else first until we come to that realization. Some of us *never* get there, and you name it, we'll try it. Shopping, drinking, drugging, cutting, exercise, sex, eating, making money, education, the list is endless, but it is all in vain. In the end, we are even more bewildered because we were so certain that was it. Oh, if only…

Jesus said, "I am the Way the Truth and the Life"(John 14:6). Deepak Chopra or Oprah can't help fill the void. Only Jesus can. I am personally fuller than I could ever have dreamed; *overflowing* is the best way to describe it. My cup runneth over. That saying never meant anything to me before. Now I get it, and I feel it!

The secular world failed to be of any help to me in my struggle to overcome my addictions because temptation—Satan's filthy grip—was too tight. I put my faith in Jesus. It was not until I surrendered, humbled myself, and begged for forgiveness, that God moved in, and Satan was defeated. I no longer live with those demonic forces that controlled me. Anyone who flat-out denies that the Holy Spirit is not living inside millions is devilishly deceived. I now understand why born-again Christians say Jesus is the only way. It is not just because the Bible says so. We, after knowing what only born-again Christians know, want it for everyone. If you have not experienced it, don't try to intellectualize it. Find it in your heart to believe what I have been called to share with you.

> And hope does not disappoint us, because God has poured out his love into our hearts by the Holy Spirit, whom he has given us. (Romans 5:5 NIV)

Having shared that scripture written by the apostle Paul, and there are so many more to corroborate my story, I must come to the conclusion that the authors of the Bible way back then, in *primitive* times, had the very same experience as I did with my *contemporary* mind. How awesome is that? It seems humans have not really changed that much. The wisdom of the Bible is timeless because of God, who was, and is, and is to come.

SISTER SOUL

I want to share with you the letter I mailed Angel on September 17, 2009, just a month after my revelation. This is the same letter I showed the Santa dude. I am including it as a useful tool. I would give similar advice to anyone wanting to strengthen their relationship with God and overcome their demons. I wrote it immediately following a phone conversation with Angel. She was in a very scary place emotionally. She sometimes would take weeks to respond to repeated phone calls and e-mails. I included with the letter a brand-new copy of Charles Stanley's *Life Principles Daily Bible*:

> Angel,
>
> You don't know how awesome it felt to talk to you today. I have so much I'd like to share with you, and I'm gonna do my best even when you live so far away. Letters, phone calls, e-mails—whatever it takes.
>
> You must heed my advice, and I promise your life will be transformed.
>
> 1. Start with this daily Bible. It has been so powerful in my life (and Kenny's too).

2. Tune into *only* Christian radio. I'm sure there are several in the area.
3. Find a Christian bookstore, and visit it frequently; it's a great way to spend your money.
4. Seek out Jesus freaks like me. Church, Bible studies, etc., when the time is right.
5. Podcasts are awesome too.

Mark Driscoll (Mars Hill Church)
Alistair Begg
Paul E. Sheppard
Joyce Meyers
Matt Chandler
Andy Stanley (Charles Stanley's son. Your Bible!)
Creflo Dollar
James MacDonald

It's time to change your focus. I realize you have little downtime, but filling it with positive God messages is the key. Soon, you will be craving it, and you won't be able to live without it. Amazingly, you will find more time and ways to fit God into your life.

In the beginning, you will shed many tears as you start connecting the dots. Purging is where it's at. I know! Tears of joy will come though, in God's time, and there is nothing like the overwhelming sense of peace that comes from a close personal relationship with God. Oh yeah, and lots of prayers. Just start talking. It does not have to be formal, and posture does not matter. You can pray on the toilet if you like!

God misses you, and *you* know it!

I can't begin to describe how much my life has changed by focusing on our beautiful Lord and Savior, Jesus Christ. He is the key to anyone's ultimate enlightenment.

I feel as though this letter is directly from God. Wow!

I don't wish to pressure you. I want only to help. And let me know if you'd like other stuff to focus on too.

There is nothing I would not do for you.

About the Bible, when you don't have time to read the entire day, just focus on the "Life Lessons," "Life Examples," "What the Bible Says About," etc. Don't feel guilty if you miss days. Just get back into it ASAP.

Please read September 9: "Life Examples: Encouragement for a Troubled Heart" immediately following this letter. It's my second anniversary of entry into rehab! It's about *you* and *me*. We are unbelievably special children of God!

God has blessed you. Let him know!

All my love and more, Amy

PS: When you're feeling down or afraid, just picture me praising the Lord in church and Kenny singing!

Time to read my Bible! It's a good thing!

Life Examples: Encouragement for a Troubled Heart

2 Corinthians 1:3-1

As a Christian, you are directed to emulate Christ. However, you can never forget that Jesus's role was of the Suffering Servant.

Second, Corinthians 1:3–4 teaches, "Blessed be the God and Father of our Lord Jesus Christ, the Father of mercies and God of all comfort, who comforts us in all our tribulations, that we may be able to comfort those who are in any trouble, with the comfort with which we ourselves are comforted by God."

If you are wondering about your sufferings, understand that you are being trained to be a servant as Jesus was. You are learning how to comfort others in the midst of their great afflictions.

It is truly an amazing and blessed thing to lift someone up in the midst of their trials and heartache. However, this cannot be done by simple exuberance and flattery. On the contrary, true, priceless encouragement can only come from a heart that has likewise suffered.

That is why in 2 Corinthians 1:6, Paul teaches, "If we are afflicted, it is for your consolation and salvation."

You have been chosen to be a blessing. Take heart in the fact that you, like our Suffering Servant Jesus, and the apostle Paul, have been afflicted for the comfort and salvation of others.

Angel was at a point where she really wanted to feel free to study the Bible openly, but unfortunately, was ridiculed by her husband and her in-laws about her faith. I could tell it was slowing down her spiritual growth and raising doubts in her mind. She still spoke of suicide, and her husband was a huge obstacle to overcome. I may have been asking too much of her at this time, so I did not push church and Bible study like I wanted to.

I asked her to read the "Life Examples" for a couple of reasons. First of all, I wanted her to know that all her suffering, wherever it was coming from, would one day be of great service to others. Whatever she was going through was not in vain. Angel was so difficult to read and a master at putting on a happy face while dying inside.

Angel has what she refers to as "the lost years." She has "no continuum," and that's very frightening. It's not fun to dredge up the past. I've never received any pleasure out of sharing my stories. It is embarrassing and painful. I'm sure Angel would prefer to never think about the past again, but it still haunts her. Most especially what she doesn't remember, I'm afraid. I was fortunate not to have blackouts. It was unacceptable for me. That was a *high* priority. Angel was not so lucky.

Secondly, I wanted her to know I could be her helper, her comforter. I understood her better than anyone else on the planet. I suffered right along with her all those years in our youth. I didn't want her to live in her pain anymore. I could help her now that I had found my salvation. I just wanted to give her a never-ending hug, God's gift of salvation through Christ. The problem was, she had to want my help.

Angel is very proud of me and aware of the enormous changes I've made. And in a meeting with her fellow teachers, when her group was asked who their hero was, she replied, "My sister," and then explained how I'd had experienced a revelation from God. When she told me the story, I was hoping she was going to tell me that Jesus was her answer. I'm sure Angel had been praying for a revelation of her own.

I can only imagine what she thought when I called her that morning to tell her that God told me to write a book. It sounds a little goofy. Now she knows because there is no denying I've been washed clean. I want it for her too.

I will elaborate on the letter with several key ingredients of my successful recovery.

My waking thought is of God. It used to be buzzables. I've obviously come a long way. I thank God for another day, praying for wisdom and discernment and read Greg Laurie's *Daily Devotional* and spend time meditating on the scripture he's included.

Getting in the habit of reading the Bible on a daily basis should be a high priority. Charles Stanley's daily format makes it so easy! Greg Laurie's *New Believer's Bible for the New Christian* is excellent, as well. God will smile down on you. I personally am a night reader. It seems to fit the night owl in me. It doesn't matter when you read it. Kenny reads his Bible and does his heavy-duty prayer in the early morning. I can't stress enough how important reading and listening to God's word is.

> I know that God's Word is sufficient. One word from him can change a nation. His word

is from everlasting to everlasting. It is through the entrance of the everlasting Word, this incorruptible seed that we are born-again and come into this wonderful salvation. Man cannot live on bread alone, but must live by every word that proceedeth out of the mouth of God. This is the food of faith. Faith cometh by hearing, and hearing by the Word of God. (Smith Wigglesworth, *Ever Increasing Faith*)

I turn on my favorite Christian radio stations whenever possible, or I plug into my iPod and listen to Christian music or sermons, lots of sermons. Sermons and music are amazing ways to fill downtime.

Shopping at a Christian bookstore is really cool too. After rehab I found a visor clip for my car with the Serenity Prayer on it, and it's a wonderful reminder.

Believe in the power of prayer and pray about everything and anything. End your prayers with "in Jesus name" as Jesus told his followers to do (John 14:13–14). There is nothing you can't take to God. He always answers in his time—yes, no, or wait. Don't give up, and make sure it's from your heart. Pray continually (1 Thessalonians 5:17).

Going to church is so important. The resources available for the suffering are priceless. Pastor Mark and Becky played a huge part in my spiritual growth, and being around other believers means you have something in common. Verbalizing your sin is a huge step in the right direction. It can be done privately with a pastor. There is something extremely powerful about sharing your transgressions. It has everything to do with honesty. The more people you are honest with, the more humbling and freeing the experience can be. Church should be a place where you can open your heart with no fear of judgment.

Service is essential. It takes the focus off of yourself and can help build a heart filled with gratitude for what you do have. Addiction is selfish. Figure out what your gifts are and use them to help others. We all have God-given gifts. Go online, and find a survey to discover your gifts if you have to. Put down the drink, the pipe, the porn, the TV remote, and the flippin' phone, and help someone today! God is watching and will not forget the love you have shown!

PREACH, PREACHER!

What if you are not sure you have a problem? I typed in "Are you an alcoholic?" on Bing for research purposes and came up with a ton of hits. Find a quiz and take it. But I must say if you have ever asked yourself the question, you may have a problem. Now is the time to seek the answer. Outright denial is a problem for many as well. I personally was quite content living in full awareness. I cringe at the thought of how many functioning addicts there are out there. It is a harsh reality.

The random quiz I took had twenty-one questions, and I answered yes to eighteen of them. This is what it said: "If you answered 'yes' to 11–20 of these, you are at high risk. Even you are no longer persuaded by the explanations you give for your drinking. Seek help from someplace other than the place where you usually go when you need help."

Great answer! It reminds me of the definition of *insanity* that I learned in AA. "Insanity is doing the same thing over and over expecting different results." Amen! I finally tried God.

The moderate category, answering yes to 4–10 stated the following: "Alcohol has probably gotten you into more trouble than you'd like. The possibility that this trend will continue is *high*."

Drinking alcohol on a regular basis, say every weekend, is a slippery slope. If you drink almost daily, you need to ask yourself why. Try to quit for a month, a week, a couple days. Well?

If you are struggling with more than one addiction, because they often come in multiples, I believe I received sound advice to stop *all* the drugs and alcohol and then focus on the cigarettes at a later date, if you indeed smoke. Otherwise, please don't fool yourself into thinking you can just keep smoking dope or do lines as long as you are not drinking or however you want to spin it. Don't get it twisted. Just get over it! God is not into torture, but get real. A drug is a drug!

I found the benefits of rehab and AA, immeasurable, because they stressed a higher power. I can't believe that any treatment without stressing something greater than ourselves will get you very far or lead to anything that lasts. In my experience, the *higher power* was the key. It was the most important aspect of my recovery. It led me to Jesus. I'd been going to church for about a year when entering rehab. I didn't believe in Jesus yet, but I had an open mind, because I was running out of options. Rehab and AA really helped me realize why a higher power was needed for my recovery.

―⁂―

I already mentioned that I did ninety AA meetings in ninety days and stayed sober. It's a huge commitment, and it was tough to do, but when you have hit rock bottom, you'll do anything to stay sober. As they say in

AA, "One day at a time," and "it works if you work it!" As soon as I quit going to meetings, I drank. So going will keep you sober, but for me, the God connection was what ultimately set me free. Free of meetings and cravings. Christianity "works if you work it" too. I love my freedom in Christ. Jesus became my sponsor!

Fellowship with other alcoholics and addicts is extremely important in the beginning. There is nothing like the nonjudgmental glance from another similarly suffering human being. The sooner you get over what everyone else thinks about you, the better. Share your story. Transparency is extremely liberating.

I get my fellowship at church now and am working on building relationships, volunteering, socializing, and attending Bible studies. My church is full of nothing but sinners. They are no better than even me in the eyes of God. Can you believe that? Isn't that awesome?

I have gone to a few AA meetings for the sake of supporting my friend Roxy who, sadly, got her second DUI. AA meetings are filled with people that are there only to get the required court papers signed, like my dear friend. It is a broken system in a broken world. I introduced her to my *home* group so she would feel more at ease. She might not be an alcoholic, but she was one of many dumb enough—me included—to get behind the wheel of a car after hitting a bar. Roxy hated the meetings and got little, if anything, out of the program. I, on the other hand, found the program educational and enjoyable in my quest for sobriety.

The last meeting I went to with Roxy was in June of 2010, ten months sober for me, and interestingly enough, one of the handouts was the only non-AA reference used in the entire AA program: How to Listen to God. It was written in the late 1930s by John E. Batterson, a personal friend of Dr. Bob's, cofounder of AA. Reverend John Batterson was pastor of a Methodist church and the Second Army chaplain. It had the Bible written all over it, just in not so many words. It is the one thing that frustrates me about AA. Jesus is not mentioned. As a Christian now, I would recommend that you find a Celebrate Recovery meeting if you can. I wish someone would have told me about them sooner. The ones I have attended start with fellowship and a meal then on to a little praise and worship time and usually a testimony, followed by small group discussion, split up by gender. AA meetings on the other hand are strictly an hour and you either listen to someone read, or go around the table and listen to those who care to share. Poor Roxy could not stand listening to people's issues.

Pastor MD has a podcast entitled "Addiction" based on Proverbs. Everyone should listen to it. There are even study questions at the end. It was extremely helpful to me. I believe Pastor MD is right on the money. I will try to summarize as best I can, as it is jam-packed. I must say, it blew my mind that the Bible is so relevant to today's issues of addiction; alcoholism included.

Pastor MD explains what the Bible says about this subject, although the terminology is different.

> The Bible speaks of idolatry. The six mentioned in Proverbs are adultery, slothfulness, greed, pride,

drunkenness, and gluttony. Idolatry is why we become addicted to things other than God. Our focus is on something other than God. Addiction should not be put in the same category as cancer. Cancer is a disease because we have no control over it. If you have a disease, you are a victim, and there is no need to repent. Addiction is a sin that you cannot seem to stop because it has great power over you. Addiction is a "worship disorder" and the Bible holds us responsible for our sin.

Pastor James MacDonald of Harvest Bible Church and Walk in the Word ministry, in his excellent "Wise up About Alcohol" sermon series shares:

> If alcohol is a disease…
> It's the only one contracted by an act of your will.
> It's the only one that requires a license to propagate it.
> It's the only disease that is bought and sold.
> It's the only one that is habit forming.
> It's the only one spread through advertising.

Pastor J Mac also says that "there are conflicting studies and the subject has not been settled on genetic predisposition. People want it to be true."

I agree with Pastor J Mac. Individual circumstances play a part. People may have an inclination to abuse drugs and alcohol. The choice is ultimately ours. To use or not to use, that is the question. I don't believe that anyone could abuse drugs and alcohol the way I did and not become addicted. I did it to myself. I made the wrong choices. I can't blame it on my last five generations of Polish descent. That would be way too easy. Alcoholics and drug addicts have to take responsibility and get to the root issue. It's one of those tough pills to swallow.

Pastor MD says,

> Idolatry is when we worship created things instead of the creator God. It is not a stretch to say that behind all idolatry are demonic forces, deception, and enslavement.

Satan is the father of lies. Satan loves it when we worship drugs, sex, money, food, or ourselves. Are you a captive, imprisoned by unhealthy desires? We are all in a constant state of worship. What is it for you?

Both Pastor MD and Pastor J Mac point out Proverbs 23:29–35.

> Who has woe? Who has sorrow? Who has needless bruises? Who has blood shot eyes?
>
> Those who linger in wine.
>
> Do not gaze at wine when it is red, when it goes down smoothly.
>
> In the end it bites like a snake and poisons like a viper.
>
> Your eyes will see strange sights and your mind imagine confusing things.
>
> You will be like one sleeping on the high seas.
>
> "They hit me," you will say, "but I'm not hurt!
>
> They beat me, but I don't feel it!
>
> When will I wake up
>
> So I can find another drink?"

That's alcoholism at its best! Pastor MD goes on to say:

> Satan is working on your mind, body, and soul. The heart is mentioned 900 times in the Bible; heart, meaning the essence. Proverbs 4:23 says, Above all else, guard your heart, for it is the wellspring of life. Culture is trying to change people's behavior, but the Bible is trying to change the person at the heart level. Any long-term freedom requires a new heart. Being born-again, giving your sin to Jesus, becoming a Christian."
>
> Proverbs 1:7 says, "The fear of the Lord is the beginning of knowledge, but fools despise wisdom and instruction." Fear of the Lord is the answer to addiction and idolatry. Fear of the Lord is this; you honor God, you love God you trust God above all else. God is God. Creator is God. Created things are not God. It is not cowering in terror, but it's this deep reverence and respect that you actually listen to God, submit to God, obey God because God's good, idols are bad. God tells the truth, idols lie. God causes life, idols bring death.

Pastor J Mac points out 1 Corinthians 6:12: "All things are lawful, but not all things are helpful. I will not be under the power of anything else."

Just because something is legal doesn't mean it is good for you. Some examples might be junk food, alcohol, prescription drugs, cigarettes, strip clubs, and pornography. These legal things are destroying minds, bodies, and souls.

"But each one is tempted when he is drawn away by his own desires and enticed. Then, when desire has conceived, it gives birth to sin; and sin, when it is fullgrown, brings forth death." (James 1:14-15)

Drunkenness and altering ones mind with drugs is sinful behavior and the result is emptiness among other things.

Another fine pastor, Andy Stanley of North Point Ministries has a fabulous sermon series called *Guard Rails*. It triggered in me another long period of sobriety. Andy Stanley probes, "In light of our past experiences, present circumstances, and future hopes and dreams, you need to ask yourself, what is the wise thing to do?" Think about it. This is a powerful question. If you have a history of alcoholism in your family, is it wise to drink? If you did happen to have a predisposition, that doesn't negate your responsibility to make a wise decision based on what you know. We have to stop making excuses for our behavior. Lord knows I had to.

EPILOGUE: LOVE IS...

I have so many things to be grateful for today that in the past I was not capable of fully appreciating. My relationship with God has taken my feeble understanding of love to a much higher level. Love never fails!

Love is...sobriety.

I am keenly aware that some struggles are more complex than others. We do not choose what we are born into, and when dealing with the extremes of wealth and poverty, the challenges become intensified.

It sickens me how the media feeds on celebrity addiction and rehab, and I have often thanked God for not being born into wealth and fame. I'm not sure I could have handled the responsibilities that come with that lifestyle. Overcoming and changing *everything* would be an extremely difficult feat, short of becoming a hermit. Whitney Houston is a prime example. Her torment ended in premature death, and Satan would like us to believe he won the battle, but it is my deep conviction that Whitney Houston is now in the arms of her heavenly Father. God is so merciful. Satan may have destroyed her physical being, but her soul belongs to Jesus. At the Grammy's and just a day after Whitney Houston's death, LL Cool J said, "We've had a death in the family." Not just the music industry, but my family too. She was a fellow sufferer of addiction, and I share a close family bond, and I cry inside when I hear any news of those overcome by their demons.

On the other side of the spectrum, I have a friend from back in my heavy cocaine and drinking days (just prior to moving to Iowa) who contacted me via Facebook, to my surprise. It had been over twenty years, and honestly, I could not believe he was still alive. I remember him practically bragging about his angels back in the day. He had three of them, and he said they were always with him. He never feared death because of them, as if he had a license to overindulge. He was one of those very scary drunks.

It was one New Year's Eve when my phone bleeped, and I received his friend request on Facebook along with a message to call him. I confirmed his request and called him (after getting Kenny's okay), shaking and praying that he was on the straight and narrow. Come to find out, he had not had a drop of alcohol in eleven years, but at age thirty-nine, he decided to try heroin. I was horrified at this news. He had been kicked out of rehab four times and, at one point, was banned from the Methadone clinic. As he was telling me what he had been through, he added that his angels were still watching over him. I couldn't believe my ears. I always thought that his angels were drunken talk. He went on to tell me that he had been heroin free for a year, and about the event that led him to his current situation. My friend lost everything due to his addictions. He burned all his bridges, as oftentimes addicts do. He couldn't keep a job and did not have a driver's license (he lost it when he was twenty-two) or a vehicle. He was living on the streets, and he had some things in a storage unit. One evening, in the dead of Michigan winter, out of heroin and out of hope, he went to visit his things at the storage unit for the last time. He was seriously contemplating suicide. Alongside the storage unit, out of the corner of his eye, he noticed a car in the creek. He jumped to action and discovered an elderly man trapped inside. He pulled him to safety, and the rest, as they say, is history. This well-to-do elderly couple was so thankful that they gave him a place to live and a job working on their Christmas tree farm. It was a miracle!

My friend, at age forty-four, is clean and sober, and I had the pleasure of introducing him to Celebrate Recovery. He is a bit isolated due to his circumstances, but he loves Jesus and is receiving financial support for counseling from the fine Christian couple that took him under their wings. Very possibly, they were two of his three angels.

I count my blessings everyday that I was able to overcome my demons.

Love is…tennis.

Keeping physically fit is a huge part of honoring God. Let my smoke-free, drug-free body be a testimony to all who suffer from lack of ambition and activity. It is never too late to pick up a sport or start exercising. I never would have dreamed that I could be good at any sport.

When I was five months sober, a tennis buddy asked me to be her partner in a local New Year's tennis tournament, my first tournament ever. We won our division and took home the trophy! I hadn't even quit smoking yet! When I was two years sober and had gone eighteen months without smoking, my travel tennis team won our district and moved on to the state championships. We wound up winning the Michigan State Championships at the 3.5 level against the odds. We went on to the Midwest section and beat Ohio and Wisconsin, but lost to Indiana and Illinois. What a blast! It was an experience I'll never forget. Tell you what, almost nothing lifts the spirits like a good sweat.

My tennis friends have been amazing. I kept no secrets after that August. If any have passed judgment on me, I am unaware; *alcoholic* and *addict* are such scary words. They were all so blindsided by the news. My tennis friends mean the world me. I love being a part of a team. It's like family. We need each other. We cheer each other on and console each other when we lose.

The coaches are awesome too! I don't know how they put up with us. Getting a dozen or more women to stop talking is a feat in itself, let alone honing our skills.

One evening during summer, about twelve of us tennis ladies enjoyed a long troll around a picturesque lake in a pontoon boat. I was the only one not drinking with a couple of stocked coolers on board. I have to admit I was having more fun than the rest. Like Dad says, "I'd have fun at a funeral!" I was passing around a mock-up of my book cover and half-jokingly said that I really should name my book "Drink, Pray, Puke." Then maybe I could have a movie too like *Eat, Pray, Love*. At least mine would have a solid ending. I found the book an enjoyable read (one of my tennis buddies suggested it) but was disappointed with the conclusion.

Love is…my clients.

I am blessed to be able to touch people in my line of work. It is a powerful position to be in. Physically touching people, as is necessary when doing hair, is as therapeutic for me as it is for my clients. I also have the ability to listen to people's stories and show compassion. It is rare that a client does not have some stressful event or past experience that has not wounded them in some way.

One of my newer clients who had recently moved from Chicago is a recovering alcoholic and relapsed after twenty years. I remember smelling alcohol on her while shampooing her one evening. Although I was privy to her long-term sobriety, I kept it to myself. She confessed to me during her following appointment a month later. My testimony and sharing my manuscript with her helped to get her back on track. I also introduced her to my AA home group, and she calls me her "sponsor"! She is a precious human being and is thankful for my understanding and compassion for those who relapse. She asked me point-blank after finishing my manuscript, "Why do you think I relapsed?" I responded quite simply, "God wasn't in the center of your life." She nodded and said, "Yep, you are absolutely right!"

This lovely lady is back on track and is into leading AA meetings and has started her very own "for women only," bless her heart!

She is far from the only suffering soul that I've ministered to in my salon thus far. I have no fear of sharing my story or my faith. The clients that I may scare off aren't the clients for me.

It is because of a client that I was guest speaker for a fellowship luncheon at a nearby church—my first speaking engagement. I spent twenty-five minutes on a small stage in front of forty lovely ladies. No fear, right? I cannot say that it was enjoyable; I started out very shaky, but the audience, if you can imagine, was extremely forgiving. I just kept telling myself that it was all for the glory of God. Glad to have that under my belt!

Love is…friendship.

Lauren and Roxy are plugging along. We all have to find our own way. There is no doubt that the Lord is working in their lives like never before. My life is finally having a positive influence. I was previously the instigator of frequent nights out at the bar. There was hardly an instance when I was not in party mode and willing to suck them into my realm of darkness. These days I am happy to report that I am being overlooked for certain functions. I am not at all excited to go and be with people whose primary goal is to tie one on. My desire to encourage that behavior has vanished.

When my friends are looking for help with a project or an ear to listen, I'm there. That's what friends are for. Over the years, for Christmas, we have exchanged token gifts. It was Christmas of 2008, when I splurged and purchased them each one my dad's small crucifixes. I never could hide my heart from these girls.

Love is…my stepchildren.

I am happy to report that Lily, Matthew, and Clare are all self-sustaining and have been very supportive and sensitive to my sobriety. Perhaps they have learned something from my collapse and rebirth. Lily came to work at the salon for a year, and I had the opportunity to share my book with her chapter by chapter. When I asked her how the book affected her, she replied, "It makes me want to go to church." That is the greatest compliment she could ever have paid me. Clare is married to a Marine and moved down South. I miss my running buddy. Matthew is following in his father's footstep's and pursuing a career as an electrician and has a lovely girlfriend! These are exciting times! My stepchildren are a blessing. They have taught me so much about my responsibilities as a parent and what it means to be an adult.

Love is…my child.

As the parent of a child in her teen years, it is up to me to prepare her for the dark side by exposing her to the light. Aubrey is well aware of my past and is all the better for it. She is now past the age when I started using drugs and walked away from church. Aubrey asked for her very own copy of Charles Stanley's *Life Principles Daily Bible*, and I surprised her when I had her name and the fish embossed on the cover. Sometimes I catch her reading it in the middle of the day. Aubrey knows what Jesus has done for me. She is in the habit of praying before she eats, even in the public school lunchroom. When she receives compliments at school on her TobyMac T-shirt or other Jesus wear, she is always very happy to report it to me. Every night, she prays a long prayer, making sure not to leave anyone out. She prays especially for my sustained sobriety and continued abstinence from smoking. Truly, how can I fail with her powerful prayers for me? We are growing together, and it is wonderful to know that Aubrey is beginning to grasp the awesomeness of God's love. I love her so, my one and only precious child, a gift from God.

> Death would be nothing without God.
> Death would be nothing without prayers.
> Death would be nothing without love.
> Our death would be just another day. (Aubrey)

I found this poem while straightening up Aubrey's room months before my revelation in August of 2009 and before her tenth birthday. My blossoming poet, she must take after Grandma Glass.

Whether or not Aubrey strays, as sheep often do, the long-term gains must be the goal: to instill in her discernment, so when Satan is knocking at the door, she will simply say, "Jesus, could you get that for me?"

Love is…my sister.

Angel's faith is growing. She is not the closet Christian she used to be; she finally started attending church. I've heard TobyMac's song "Hold On" as the ring-back on her cell phone, and she told me for the first time that she believes in Jesus as her Lord and Savior. Angel has a newfound freedom in her voice, but Satan is still on the attack, and her battle continues.

While still living down south and planning a visit to Michigan, Angel asked if she could stay with us. That was music to my ears. Angel came regularly to see her son, but since my revelation, I felt as if she was avoiding me. I was not the party girl I used to be. Her daughter lived locally, and they could spend some of the time partying. This visit was a blessing. With Angel's daughter living out of state, my home was again an option. She also asked that I would help her not drink on this trip! That I could do! It was a huge step for her to even suggest that alcohol might be a negative in her life.

Kenny and I had already made plans to take Aubrey that Saturday to Greg Laurie's Chicago Harvest Crusade about three hours away. Angel and her twelve-year-old son agreed to come. She brought along a new CD with her current favorite song, "Born Again," by the News Boys. We jammed to the CD on the way to Chicago, and I shared songs from my iPod, mostly Warren Barfield and one my favorite songs, "Unleashed" from his *Reach* album, not to mention "Come Alive," the first Christian song I remember giving me the overwhelming sense of being born-again.

Greg Laurie's sermon on the meaning of life moved Angel and the Katinas, Kirk Franklin, and Skillet jammed. Angel did not give a public profession of faith as I encouraged her to do, but she did take the kids down to the floor to get copies of Greg's *New Believers Bible for New Christians*. It was a powerful night of worship. One I will not soon forget.

Over the years, Angel has remembered me with heartfelt gifts. She has such a generous spirit, always trying to make up for the past, it seems. That visit, she gave me a CD, Francesca Battistelli's *My Paper Heart*, and said the song "Beautiful, Beautiful" was meant for me. Angel, *you* are so beautiful. I love her with all my heart. She told me in an e-mail that she can feel things changing! Angel is an incredibly strong woman, and I will always continue to support and encourage her on her walk with God.

Love is…my mother.

She has made it a tradition to compose a Christmas poem, and my "Insight" folder is loaded. Mom's gift of poetry has been a blessing to me, and I feel it appropriate to share two that have touched me deeply. To this day, I cannot read these without a stream of tears running down my face.

A MARY CHRISTMAS MEDITATION

From Eve to goddess to Jezebel,
The power of the feminine has cast a spell.
Confused by his attraction, feeling ambivalent,
Man fails to understand that
She's both counterpoint and compliment.
A true friend and mate.
Instead, he seeks to conquer and dominate.
This inexplicable tyranny over his human counterpart
Divides and destroys love like a stake through the heart.

I believe that our Creator designed a woman's role

To bring balance to creation and make mankind whole.
Why else would He choose a humble, unassuming girl
To bring His Gift of Love into the world
And By virtue of this wondrous birth,
Forever affirm her gender's worth?
For as the universal portal through
Which life and knowledge emanate'
She holds the seeds of possibility, our fate.

(Rose Mary Glass, 2005)

The Unherald Hero of Christmas

In the familiar narrative of Christmas,
A heroic figure vanished without notice.
Amid the spectacle of Angel choruses,
Mysterious stars and Eastern kings'
Forgotten is a man of quiet courage
Whose praises no one sings.

Who stood by the pregnant maiden?
Who knocked on doors seeking shelter, in vain?
Who gave support and comfort, waited patiently
As she labored through the wondrous night?
Who then whisked the family off to Egypt,
In furtive flight?

It was Joseph a carpenter, the husband of Mary,
But not the Boy's father, it is said,
Who took on the mantle of parent,
Provider and protector, taught Jesus his trade,
Took Him to temple, who sets
A true moral example.

In these times of irresponsible paternity,

Philandering, abuse, and infidelity,
Where are the models of real manhood to be found?
Surely not in celebrity athletes, powerful politicians'
Financial magnates, greedy CEOs or priests.
Hypocrites all to say the least.
Lest we again overlook the obvious,
Consider all the Josephs who exist in our midst.
The regular Joes, who respect women,
Honor their duty as husbands, fathers, and sons.
Men who deserve respect and admiration.
Not superstars but *wholly* men.

(Rose Mary Glass, 2009)

I don't know how she does it. All of her poems stir up so much emotion in me. She is a woman filled with love and passion. She gave her children her all when we were little, and she still touches my heart today. Love you, Mom! You are the best!

Love is… my dad, the artist.
Oh, the mornings he woke me up yelling, "Rise and shine for the Great Lakes line!" He learned that the first summer after high school graduation working as a porter sailing on the Great Lakes. I am not a morning person and never found it very funny, but you gotta love the man. His artwork has obviously had a profound effect on my life. He has held Jesus close to heart, and that fact has permeated his being. His passion, aside from his sculpture and ceramics, is for his children, that we find happiness, and his heart has been heavily burdened by his children's suffering. My dad composed a letter to all his children shortly after my stay in rehab,

apologizing for his casual treatment of alcohol in his home. He may have some regrets and maybe he didn't always do the right things, but I never doubted his love for me. I think one of the greatest compliments a daughter could pay her father is to want to someday marry someone like him. Dad set the bar pretty high.

Love is… Kenny, my Joseph.

I thank God for my skills of painting. Otherwise, Kenny might have never found the courage to call me. I have Kenny to thank for being that man to lead me back to church. He was placed in my path for that purpose. It is a beautiful thing, Kenny and me. One of our favorite things to do together is listening to sermon podcasts. I don't think it will ever get old. Whether in the car or cruising on the Harley, we just try to keep our focus on the kingdom of God. That is not to say that we don't have our issues like all couples do. I still struggle with self-esteem, and it is a real battle in our culture. I am trying to keep my foot out of my mouth, but it is always a challenge. I continue to apologize, repent, and pray for forgiveness.

One of the couples that went on a mission trip to Kentucky with us is modeling what we would someday like to do: disaster relief efforts and Habitat for Humanity around the country. The needs are endless, and we long to use our handy gifts. Kenny is willing to do just about anything along the construction line, and I love playing apprentice, and if there is painting to do, give me a brush and a roller, and I am good to go.

Kenny is the love of my life, and he gave up drinking altogether at about my two-year sober mark—no pressure from me, but as a way to honor his wife and the Lord. I have a husband with a heart of gold, and I will take Dad's advice and continue to try really hard not to screw this one up!

Love is…Jesus, the ultimate high, *the* almighty buzz. Jesus said:

> Come to me, all who are weary and burdened, and I will give you rest. Take my yoke upon you and learn from me, for I am gentle and humble in heart, and you will find rest for your souls. For my yoke is easy and my burden is light.
>
> Matthew 11:28–30

Immanuel means "God is with us." The Conquering Spirit dwells within the believer and gives us the strength to overcome. The Lord sent the Holy Spirit to be our helper and comforter; The Father, Son, and the Holy Spirit. What an awesome plan!

And as for my conclusion:

It was a gorgeous, cool, crisp sunny fall morning. Kenny was on a men's retreat with his big brother, and I was watching Aubrey play her last soccer game of the season. No cooler behind my seat, no beer in my mug, no guzzling at halftime. No sitting in the car, getting stoned or sucking down smokes and watching from a distance. I was free to sit on the sideline, no longer confined by my addictions.

While watching the game, I was listening to Pastor MD's "Addiction" podcast again in preparation for working on my book. Oddly enough, the podcast wound up being number one on my song list, so afterward, I decided to go down the A-list, and see what was worth listening to. Not all the songs were Christian like on the special playlists I was accustomed to the last couple years. I skipped over several songs until I came to Chris Tomlin's rendition of "Amazing Grace." Next was a guitar solo and instrumental of "Amazing Grace" by Carlos Santana and Jeff Beck. I wasn't even aware that the song "American Pie" by Don McLean was on my iPod. (Kenny's in charge of i-Tunes.)

Don McLean had always been one of my favorites back in the day. His song, "Vincent (Starry, Starry Night)" had special meaning to me because of my dad, the artist, and my appreciation of Vincent van Gogh. I remembered that "American Pie" had some God and Satan in it, so instead of blowing by it, I decided to listen, and the final verse hit me really hard. "The Father, Son, and the Holy Ghost, they caught the last train for the coast the day the music died." I began to cry. Luckily, I was wearing my sunglasses. I don't think anyone noticed, but just the thought of the absence of God and the sounds of praise and worship, the music of our souls, completely overwhelmed me. What a tragedy that would be.

I can't even begin to imagine this world without Jesus and God's Word. I no doubt would have died a pathetic drunk, probably with a cigarette in one hand, a beer in the other, and stoned to boot. Not the legacy of an exalted life. Lord knows we need a savior. Rest assured, he will never leave or forsake us.

I was having a moment, and then the next song on the list started to play, and I couldn't resist sharing it with you because it is all for the glory of God. "Audience of One" by Big Daddy Weave.

> And now, just to know you more
> Has become my great reward...

Now is the time to get your priorities in order. The most important decision you will ever make is your decision to follow Jesus or not. Let my book be a testimony to the power that the gospel had on my life. Can I get a witness? Nothing compares to the eternal high I have now. Jesus first, and everything else will fall into place. You too can experience God's unfailing love and amazing grace. In the movie *Letter's to God*, Tyler, the boy dying of cancer said, "I just want everyone to believe." Me too, I have to share the good news. The cure for addiction is Christ alone.

And if you recall, my father's firstborn son and my big brother's name is Christopher, as well as the name of my very first love that died *because of me*. I find those facts absolutely stunning. The Greek meaning of *Christopher* is "bearing Christ inside," and need I mention my dad's artwork or that I am *beloved*, the meaning of my name? He's been a part of my life from the very beginning, just some friendly reminders, I suppose. "Yes, Jesus loves me, for the Bible tells me so." Now I know! What a blessing to be born with *Jesus in my face*.

The End

AMY'S PLAYLIST

Afters
-"Light Up the Sky"

Amy Grant
-"Better Than a Hallelujah"

Addison Road
-"What Do I Know of Holy"

Aaron Shust
-"Give Me Words to Speak"
-"My Savior My God"
-"My Hope Is in You"

Audio Adrenaline
-"My Father's House"

Barlow Girls
-"Never Alone"
-"Enough"

Bebo Normam
-"I Will Lift My Eyes"
-"Here Goes"

Big Daddy Weave
-"Every Time I Breathe"
-"Audience of One"
-"What Life Would Be Like"

Brandon Heath
-"I'm Not Who I Was"
-"Our God Reigns"
-"Love Never Fails"
-"Give Me Your Eyes"
-"Your Love"

Brit Nicole
-"All This Time"
-"The Lost Get Found"

Building 429
-"You Carried Me"

Casting Crowns
-"East to West"
-"Slow Fade"
-"Every Man"

Chasen
-"On and On"

Chris August
-"7 × 70"
-"Starry Night"
-"Battle"

Chris Tomlin
-"Amazing Grace"
-"Holy Is the Lord"
-"I Will Rise"
-"God of This City"

Fireflight
-"Unbreakable"
-"He Weeps"

Franchesca Battistelli
-"Beautiful, Beautiful"

Heather Williams
-"Hallelujah"

Hillsong
-"Hosanna"

Jamie Grace
-"You Lead"

Jars of Clay
-"Out of My Hands"

Jeremy Camp
-"Lay Down My Pride"
-"This Man"
-"There Will Be a Day"

Jonny Diaz
-"Stand For You"
-"More Beautiful You"

Josh Wilson
-"Savior Please"

Jason Gray
-"Remind Me Who I Am"

Katinas
-"Thank You"

Kirk Franklin
-"Revolution"
-"He Reigns"
-"Stomp"

Kutless
-"Strong Tower"
-"What Faith Can Do"

Laura Story
-"Mighty to Save"
-"Blessings"

Leeland
-"Be Lifted High"
-"Tears of the Saints"

Lifehouse
-"Beautiful (Everything)"
-"Hanging by a Moment"

Lincoln Brewster
-"Salvation Is Here"

Mandisa
-"Shackles"
-"My Deliverer"
-"Voice of a Savior"
-"He Is With You"

Matthew West
-"You Are Everything"
-"The Motions"
-"Strong Enough"
-"My Own Little World"

Matt Maher
-"Turn Around"

Mercy Me
-"Bring the Rain"
-"All of Creation"
-"You Reign"
-"Hold Fast"

Natalie Grant
-"I Will Not Be Moved"
-"I'm in Better Hands Now"

News Boys
-"Born Again"
-"He Reigns"

Nichole Nordeman
-"Holy"
-"Finally Free"
-"Brave"

Nicole C. Mullen
-"Redeemer"
-"Call on Jesus"

Phillips, Craig, and Dean
-"Revelation Song"
-"Your Name"
-"When the Stars Burn Down"

Pillar
-"Hindsight"
-"Indivisible"
-"Frontline"

Pocket Full of Rocks
-"Alive"

Point Of Grace
-"How You Live"

Rebecca St. James
-"Pray"
-"Song of Love"

Remedy Drive
-"Speak to Me"

Rich Mullens
-"Awesome God"

Rush of Fools
-"Can't Get Away"
-"Undo"

Sanctus Real
-"Forgiven"
-"I'm Not Alright"
-"Whatever You're Doing"

Sara Groves
-"When the Saints"
-"Add to the Beauty"

Skillet
-"Hero"
-"Rebirthing"
-"Better than Drugs"
-"Awake and Alive"

Steven Curtis Chapman
-"Live Out Loud"
-"I'm Diving In"

Superchick
-"Pure"
-"Stand in the Rain"

Switchfoot
-"Mess of Me"
-"We Are One Tonight"
-"Awakening"

Tenth Avenue North
-"Healing Begins"
-"By Your Side"
-"Love Is Here"

Third Day
- "Revelation"
- "Run to You"
- "Here I Am to Worship"
- "Children of God"
- "Lift Up Your Face"

TobyMac
- "Truth"
- "Made to Love"
- "One World"
- "Hold On"
- "J-Train"
- "Throw Yo Hands Up"

Vota
- "Honestly"
- "Hard to Believe"

Warren Barfield
- "Love Is Not a Fight"
- "Saved"
- "Come Alive"
- "Unleashed"